THE VICTORIAN ROMANTICS

The Two Sleepers and the One that Watcheth

Simeon Solomon

THE VICTORIAN ROMANTICS

1850-70

*The Early Work of Dante Gabriel Rossetti, William
Morris, Burne-Jones, Swinburne, Simeon
Solomon and their Associates*

BY

T. EARLE WELBY

ARCHON BOOKS
Hamden, Connecticut
1966

Originally Published 1929

Reprinted 1966 by arrangement with
THE BODLEY HEAD LTD.
in an unaltered and unabridged edition

Library of Congress Catalog Card Number: 66-15389
Printed in the United States of America

My dear Wise,—The grandchildren of an eminent Victorian novelist delighted Swinburne by their confident assumption that their ancestor's stories had been written expressly and exclusively for them. Well, when I find in the incomparable Ashley Library precisely the first editions and manuscripts which I need, I feel inclined to assume that, decades before our acquaintance began, you collected all those rarities for me! Certainly, the generosity with which you throw open your collection to me encourages a belief otherwise not very obviously reasonable. I can make you no adequate return for hours in the most interesting and hospitable room in London, for the excitement of having in my hands the treasures you have brought together in your long devotion to the writers whom I also peculiarly cherish. But accept this book, and believe me

Ever yours
T. EARLE WELBY

LIST OF ILLUSTRATIONS

LIST OF ILLUSTRATIONS

**
*

The Author and the Publishers wish to acknowledge with gratitude their obligations to all who have facilitated the use of the pictures and manuscripts illustrated in this volume, and in particular to Mr T. J. Wise, the authorities of the Victoria and Albert Museum, Messrs Morris and Mr Frederick Hollyer

THE VICTORIAN ROMANTICS

I

AN account of the Romantic Movement in English poetry is only too apt to be arbitrary in choice of a starting-point. Consider the Movement as a whole, and who shall say exactly where it begins? With Chatterton, if you like, with Blake, with the publication of the *Lyrical Ballads*. But there had been dim beginnings much earlier, a kind of ' return to nature ' with Dyer so far back as 1726, when he issued ' Grongar Hill,' a return with Thomson not only to nature, sometimes so closely observed as in the description of the autumnal sun that ' sheds, weak and blunt, his wide-refracted ray,' but to so purely Romantic a poet as Spenser. However it may have seemed to contemporaries and may still seem to conventional historians of literature, the eighteenth-century ideal was menaced almost before it was fully established. On the other hand, by a happy paradox which should not have escaped the notice of critics, the two perfect lyrics of the eighteenth century, the two pieces in which the finest possibilities allowed by those limiting conditions are realized, were written by Romantic poets, by Blake in ' To the Muses,' by Coleridge in ' Youth and Age.'

But if it would be difficult to know quite where to begin a critical record of the Romantic Movement as a whole, there is no difficulty in deciding where to begin this book on *The Victorian Romantics*. Chronologically, Tennyson and Browning come well within the period. Both outlived Rossetti, and nearly all the finest work of Morris and Swinburne was done well before the last volumes of the two elder poets appeared. During the greater part of the Queen's reign Tennyson was officially and popularly regarded

3

as sovereign of song, and Browning was the idol of, at any rate, a considerable circle of Victorian intellectuals. Both were eminently Romantic in all their better work, though with Browning there was that frequent tendency towards the overbalanced Romanticism which yields us the grotesque. But neither comes into this argument. For in their Romanticism they date back. Extremely Victorian as they, and especially Tennyson, may be in other respects, as Romantics they are pre-Victorian, Tennyson being a poet to whom Keats is a recent discovery, Browning one who has lately discovered Shelley. The Romantic work truly characteristic of the new era comes from men at least twenty years younger, from Dante Gabriel Rossetti, William Morris, Swinburne, and from a writer whose influence was felt in poetry a little earlier, Christina Rossetti.

Before the date with which I begin, say 1850, there has not in strictness been any movement. The Lake School, if it has to accommodate Southey, is a fiction; and though for a time, unhappily short, Wordsworth and Coleridge react on each other, and though Shelley mourns Keats, and though Keats for a year or two apes Leigh Hunt, these men are very much going their own ways. Tennyson and Browning work in isolation. But after 1850 there is something more than a general tendency. Not that we get with the Pre-Raphaelites, or with the little urbane group of the late 'seventies, or with the little decadent group of the 'nineties, the equivalent of religious or political movements. We shall never find that in the history of literature or art, where the aim is always, in however cordial an agreement on general principles, the self-expression of the individual, the conveying of a personal sense of the world, not the attainment of an exterior goal which exists in precisely the same form for each one of those striving towards it. But for a good many years at any rate the associates of Rossetti hold together, and those later and smaller groups also cohere.

Movements are rather un-English, and this Victorian movement, begun under an Italianate man of genius, proceeds with many exotic stimulants. In Tennyson, Europe barely exists; Browning wanders in imagination over much of it, but only for settings and situations; with Rossetti, Morris and Swinburne, and Swinburne especially, the insular mind is exposed eagerly to every alien prompting. And presently what Tennyson, in an absurd phrase, called poisonous honey stolen from France becomes the staple food of some of the men of the 'nineties.

Another distinction between this Victorian Romanticism and that represented, in their several ways, by Tennyson and Browning: from 1850 onwards, as never before, poetry is associated with, often inspired by, the graphic arts. Rossetti is not more evidently the dominant figure in the first two decades than Aubrey Beardsley in the last, and in the interval we are frequently sent from the page of poetry to the decorative art of William Morris, the paintings of Burne-Jones, the corrupt delicacies of Simeon Solomon, the lithographs and etchings of Whistler, the fans designed by Charles Conder.

Again, it is only after 1850, and in these new developments, that we find, a phenomenon much rarer with us than in France, at every stage an accredited exponent of the innovations. Before 1850 there is only Ruskin, sympathetic towards Pre-Raphaelitism, but detached from Tennyson and Browning; a little later there is Matthew Arnold, sapping Philistinism, but of no particular service to those poets. But after the first successes of Rossetti's circle they have Walter Pater, and in the 'eighties there is the witty, impudent, often suggestive popularizer Oscar Wilde, and in the 'nineties the authentic criticism of Mr Arthur Symons.

Differentiated in all these ways from the broader and vaguer Romanticism of the preceding half-century, Victorian Romanticism differs in this also, that it came much more rapidly to its climax, and not only because a long line of poets had prepared conditions favourable to its triumph. Certain of the historians of literature tend to forget that they have to take account not only of what is called genius but of character. If, as has been seen, the progress of Romanticism was so long delayed in the eighteenth century, it was not merely because the powerful influence of Pope was hostile to it. Not one of the poets in whom we see the first hints of a new feeling for nature, a new care for atmosphere or music, had the qualities which make the effective revolutionary. Gray was fastidious, frugal in production, very anxious not to be considered a working author; Thomson was mild and indolent; Collins, a withdrawn nature, gathered up his work to keep it from the public, and passed soon into the shadow of madness. They were all men of subdued vitality, little disposed to insist publicly on the value of what was novel in their somewhat tentative work. But, when we come to the Victorian Romantics, we find them led by a man who was born to command. Before insomnia and chloral broke him down, Rossetti had, as hardly anyone else in our literature has had, that casual, compelling authority, that easy, dominating way with men which marks a supreme leader. And several of his most distinguished associates were men eminently qualified to challenge accepted ideas. The tireless and many-sided effort of William Morris to renew the golden age was accompanied by the more spasmodic assaults which the high-strung and mischief-loving genius of Swinburne made on the established order—moral, political and æsthetic; and in the controversies which raged over ' The Fleshly School of Poetry ' it was made very evident that the group was capable of defending itself and ready to carry the war into the country of its opponents.

It had, of course, the usual apathy to cope with, and beyond that some stubborn prejudice against the somewhat un-English quality of emotion in much of its work. On the whole, however, its chief difficulty, in poetry, was the influence of Tennyson. Odd as it may sound, it would have been easier for the new poetry, which derived in part from Tennyson's own sources, and was, in certain instances, affected by his own earlier work, to have made way if Tennyson had been altogether in the enemy's camp. Overshadowing all contemporaries as markedly as Pope had done in the preceding century, Tennyson offered to new developments a passive resistance the harder to overcome because he frequently and discreetly adjusted himself to change. He did not present an antithesis to the new poetry: he seemed rather to show exactly how far a consummate artist in poetry who was also an Englishman and a man with a just sense of moral obligations should go along the new paths. It is true that in some portions of his work, then the least generally esteemed, he had gone further than it beseemed an idol of the mid-Victorian middle class to travel, and had revealed, for the very few who could see it, the animosities and fears and acrid discontents which were his finest inspirations. But that Tennyson, the author of *Maud* among lesser things, was by no means the Laureate revered by the pundits and the populace. The officially and popularly applauded Tennyson was more than a great poet; he was the Poet, as Victoria was the Queen. He seemed as permanent as she, rather later, came to seem. He had survived, and was to survive, so many things. There had been all that excitement, short-lived but really very considerable, over the Spasmodics. Well, if you cared for that sort of thing, there was his *Maud*. But the wiser minds, as they were deemed, rather passed by *Maud* to dwell on the general mass of his idyllic, elegiac, descriptive and meditative poetry. The contemplation of it was soothing. It left the most of those who read it with a feeling that this was final, that there could be nothing of high importance beyond it. Theoretically, they might be liberal enough to allow all sorts of possibilities; but in practice they were unwilling to believe that anything going beyond Tennyson was other than specialized and more or less eccentric, probably unwholesome, art.

And this Tennysonian influence, for several decades so paralysing to poetry, was most dangerous to the ways of dealing with the past which Rossetti, Morris and Swinburne preferred. For Tennyson had subtly modernized the great body of wild and ancient legends out of which he made what Swinburne wickedly called the Morte d'Albert. Consciously or unconsciously, he had persistently ignored the difference between medieval and Victorian sentiment, and had presented the characters of a part chivalrous, part barbaric past as refined and conscientious members of modern English society. When Morris produced, with incomparably more truth and vividness, though with a then uncertain technique, the miraculous pictures of medieval life in the *Defence of Guenevere* volume, the effect for most readers, though it was years before many found the book, could only be one of wilful perversity. When, later on, Swinburne in *Chastelard* revived with exquisite fidelity the fantastic and suicidal ardour of a mode of love well understood by choice spirits of the Renaissance, he could only be regarded as gratuitously dabbling in insane sensuality.

In regard to painting, Rossetti's circle met with no such difficulty. The work of the painters then most in fashion was evidently at most points antithetical to theirs, and the fight, arduous and prolonged as it was, was simple. Moreover, the painters in the circle included a man so accommodating as Millais, whereas not one of the poets ever made any concession to average British expectations.

It is not my purpose here to write a history of Victorian Romanticism from its emergence about 1850 to its evaporation in the little movement of the 'nineties. There are histories enough of Pre-Raphaelitism, and at the other extreme the period of Aubrey Beardsley has been quite fully enough treated. What I have proposed to myself is to study Victorian Romanticism in the origins of its several phases, and especially in those periodicals the *Germ*, the *Oxford and Cambridge Magazine*, *Undergraduate Papers*, in which challenges were thrown out to the orthodox. It is in the early work of successive generations of writers and painters or draughtsmen, in their coterie publications, and in certain polemical writings that, for the most part, I intend to study the Victorian Romantics. And since some of the documents, vaguely cited by everyone, are not quite to everyone's hand, some items indeed being very rare, I propose to quote from them freely.

What should result is not a chronicle covering the whole career of all these men of genius and talent, but a series of critical miniatures exhibiting them at or soon after the moment of entry into the movement. However necessary my allusions to the subsequent work of these men, my main concern is with their initial efforts, with them in youth, in the first rapture of innovation. I seek to present them not with the prestige of their whole achievement, but as they originally appeared to the public of their day.

My method is to take them as individuals, as they come naturally to mind. To aim at an effect of ordered critical narrative would be to secure approval in certain quarters at the cost of injustice to these poets and painters. The movement in which they took part was not something exterior and irresistible ; it was made by them, so far as each for a longer or shorter time, and of his own volition, entered into it. They are not mere illustrations of an artistic tendency emanating from a source external to them: they are artists each with his birthright, each with a will of his own, electing to join the movement each at its own hour. Chronology, that logic which is so much stricter than life or art, must not be suffered to give a false orderliness to this account of them. They matter ultimately as individuals, and must not be reduced to being mere members of a school, or so manipulated as to become a procession leading to one and the same precisely definable objective.

II

KEATS died in 1821, Shelley in 1822; and though Coleridge lived on to 1834 and Wordsworth to 1850, the first phase of the Romantic movement in England ended with the close of the second decade of the century. There followed a period during which Tennyson and Browning were developing in secret, but in which the only new poetic figures discernible by contemporaries were those of George Darley and Thomas Lovell Beddoes.

Darley, to borrow the famous phrase of Dekker's eulogist, ' had poetry enough for anything.' 'Nepenthe' is rich to excess in imagination, and of romantic strangeness. But, a fine and unsparing critic of himself as well as other men, Darley has explained his failure better than anyone else can, summing up his genius as ' occasional, intermittent, collapsive.' Lacking direction, 'Nepenthe' remains an extraordinary when it might have been a great poem. His plays, uninviting to the general reader, faintly disappointing as they must be even to a sympathetic and collaborating mind, are of finer quality than is generally allowed, and with those of Robert Landor seem to me the most unfairly neglected dramatic work of their period. But, so often on the verge of achievement, Darley achieves only in the lyric which deceived Palgrave, in the touching lines to Helene, in the beautifully metred lines which were Meredith's model for ' Love in the Valley.' To read him is to be reminded, if one ever has seen that sight, of fireflies in their uncertain morrice through a tropical grove: innumerable little lights glimmer out, but nowhere is there illumination enough for more than a momentary glimpse of leaf and flower.

Beddoes, with a yet rarer genius, is still more self-defeated, squandering his powers on a morbid, fundamentally undramatic drama on the Elizabethan model. Outside the lyrics every one knows, he can rise to wonderful passages. But, on the whole, he remains a curiosity, a carver of death's-heads which would have more value for us if they were the final sardonic comment in a comprehensive criticism of life instead of being the initial and terminal ornaments of every page. He is an architect of the house of life who can plan only the mortuary and the gargoyles.

Two other poets, born considerably later, and indeed the one twenty and the other fifteen years younger than Tennyson, came into prominence, burst into it violently, before Tennyson was universally acclaimed or Browning at all widely honoured. There is this to be said for the Spasmodics, that rashly as they strained after the sublime and insecure as they were, grandeur was not unnatural to them. Alexander Smith has worn ill, and is now perhaps remembered by little but 'Barbara,' with its echoing music, and the poem on Glasgow, which accumulates natural detail with some of the energy and success of Christopher Smart. Sydney Dobell's finest poem, 'Keith of Ravelston,' which should, however, be read in its context and not as ordinarily presented in anthologies, is a familiar possession, often and not unjustly praised as coming nearer than anything else in our poetry to 'La Belle Dame Sans Merci.' What to my mind has long seemed his next most remarkable success, 'Isabel,' has been passed over alike by anthologists and, so far as I can remember, critics and literary historians. A lament for one who can be thought upon only in the purity and peace of dawn, it has a singular delicacy of matutinal atmosphere, and is at once intimate and aloof. On a much lower level, with that realism which issued also in his own sonnets, most strikingly in the unfair assault on us of the lines in which the woman at home makes music 'for him who cannot hear the raven croaking at his carrion ear,' Dobell has another success in ' Tommy's Dead.' It is a poem of effect, competing with recitation pieces, but it does what none of its competitors has done, it renders exactly the garrulity of stricken old age.

There was upon Dobell, as upon so many other poets of his day, the curse of having no form in the larger sense; 'Balder,' with so much really beautiful incidental poetry, is a shapeless and drifting composition. They have their occasional successes, these poets, but between the death of Shelley and the full emergence of Tennyson and Browning there is hardly anywhere a volume of definitely achieved poetry. It looks as if the Romantic Movement were about to end in curious or violent but always uncertain efforts to right or left of the main course.

If anywhere there is a considerable mass of verse in which something is done to the measure of its author's intention, it is in a book not taken seriously then or now, but one which any sensitive and unprejudiced mind must, I venture to think, regard with real respect. Because the *Ingoldsby Legends* are full of laughter, because their metrical art is *funambulesque* and their rhymes the most ingeniously contrived that we have, many readers have not perceived how romantic, at moments how sinister, is this strange, often jolly, sometimes terrified, game played with mystery and horrors. Superficially, Barham goes back to monkish things and old legends to mock at them, and no doubt there is in him something of a crude, modern and Protestant desire to get a laugh out of monasticism and superstition. But beneath that, and likely enough not under his control, there is an instinct for the *macabre* rarer than that of Beddoes, and a really poetic imagination breaks out now and then, terrifyingly, though the hearty romping is immediately resumed for our reassurance and his own. Hidden away in this rollicking verse there is real feeling for at least certain aspects of that past to which nearly all the Romantics have yearned, and at the same time there is an appreciation, furtive and quickly laughed off, of some

12

things that will hardly be prized again till we are in the decadence. There are moments in the reading of the *Ingoldsby Legends*, if one is reading with a mind free from prepossessions, when one seems to be watching, in a monk's refectory transformed into a private theatre, the queer gambols of a single actor, very conscious of his solitariness, a priest-Pierrot. He walks the tight-rope infallibly, goes through his tricks at a great rate, and rattles along with his ingenious and preposterous patter, but there are dreadful things waiting to burst in from the wings, and he knows it. If he should stop romping and laughing!

During the interval between the first and the second phase of Romanticism in England, say, roughly, between a little after 1820 and a little after 1840, there had begun in France a feverish and magnificent revival of Romance. Its interest for us here lies in the fact that it anticipated that close association between the arts which was to distinguish Victorian from Georgian and Regency Romanticism. To some extent the way had been prepared for it by Rousseau; by Mme de Staël's discovery of Germany, also; but the strongest impulse came from two English writers, from Scott and from Byron, the one made amply available to French readers from 1816, the other from 1819. The supreme development of Romantic painting in France sprang from a purely pictorial source, also English; from Constable, three of whose pictures, including 'The Hay Wain,' were shown in the momentous Salon of 1824. But Romanticism had earlier issue in French painting in the work of figure painters who took their subjects or their sentiments directly or indirectly from Scott and Byron, and the influence of those two English writers, or perhaps rather the atmosphere created by certain of their French admirers, affected all the arts. If Victor Hugo appeared as part author of *Amy Robsart*, Delacroix depicted the ' Barque of Don Juan ' and ' Marino Faliero,' and Berlioz began with a *Waverley Overture* to proceed with work on a Byronic theme.

In England, however, there could be no similar movement. Scott and Byron did not, and could not, mean so much to the choicer spirits of the younger generation in England. From Scott they could get little but the accessories of Romance, and the reaction against the histrionic Romanticism of Byron had already begun. As regards poetry, the younger men in England were feeling towards a just attitude to Wordsworth, Coleridge, Shelley, Keats. The work of Wordsworth, of Coleridge, notoriously needed sifting, a task not completed until it was done by Matthew Arnold in the one instance and Swinburne in the other. Shelley, of whose volumes only one, *The Cenci*, had passed into a second edition in his own life-time, was not to be read fully till his widow finished her editorial labours in 1839. Keats had to wait till Monckton Milnes put forth the first collected edition.[1] This last, published in the vitally important year 1848, by an agreeable and suggestive coincidence was blind-blocked with the same design that appears on the fourth edition of Tennyson's *Poems*, 1846. In 1848 Rossetti's enthusiasm over Holman Hunt's work arose, as Hunt has recorded, partly from their common interest in Keats, a poet, however, very much more to Rossetti's purpose than Hunt's: they felt themselves to be exceptional in going to him for pictorial suggestions.

---

[1] There had, however, previously been published, in Smith's Standard Library, ' The Poetical Works of John Keats,' 1840; and still earlier, Galignani's ' Poetical Works of Coleridge, Shelley and Keats,' Paris, 1829. Both, of course, want the matter which gave peculiar importance to the edition of 1848.

III

IT was not that English painting was unliterary. With Leslie, a capable painter, as one recognizes when dislike of his sardine-tin surfaces has been set aside, it was only too literary. But in the anecdotal kind of painting there had been since Wilkie very little painter's notice of character and humour. Leslie and his rivals went to Shakespeare only as actors of the period rendered him, and for the rest went to Goldsmith or Sterne, not to the poets. There was, or until lately had been, imagination enough in English painting of other kinds, in the great masters of landscape. In 1848 Constable had been dead for thirteen years, but De Wint had still a year, Turner three years, and David Cox eleven years of life. Outside landscape there was imagination at work, never more nobly than in Cotman's ' The Centaur,' a drawing of surely the very highest excellence. And there was even an approach to poetry, as represented by a particular poet, in the work of Edward Calvert (1799-1883), who continued the slighter part of William Blake's pastoral work, and sometimes with that happy and personal sense of design that delights us in ' The Cyder Press.' But, broadly, painting was aloof from poetry.

The painter who had been most in the company and in the thoughts of poets was that stupendous self-deceiver, Benjamin Haydon. The writer of verse who was most zealous about painting was no poet, but the witty, malicious and generous Samuel Rogers. Landor had long ago brought a lofty yet homely sculptor's realism into poetry, in 'Gebir' especially, and Keats had done painter's work in poetry; but, on the whole, even had the artists been well aware of the poets, there could have been little imaginative commerce.

15

Painting was in that condition in which there is a paralysing general agreement as to the extent to which the ordinary phenomena are to be observed and stressed. The sudden challenge from the Pre-Raphaelites was so effective precisely because it was directed against this paralysing and unpoetic agreement. There were a great many other things in Pre-Raphaelitism besides that which inspired and roughly justified its title. And if its method, in 1848-1852, is to be regarded as the essential thing, Holman Hunt himself must be deposed in favour of a senior who was a total outsider and had long been absent from England: J. F. Lewis (1805-1876). It is not only that Lewis anticipates the passion for detail; he surpasses every Pre-Raphaelite in getting out of the method all that it can yield.

But the method, which was permanently congenial only to Holman Hunt out of all the Pre-Raphaelites, was what at the outset made the challenge effective. We are, however, thoroughly justified in allowing Holman Hunt and Millais to drop early out of our argument here, and in insisting on the leadership of Rossetti, because in the two essential things, in poetry and in independence of painter's convention, Rossetti was so very much richer.

There are revolutions which can be carried through only by an alien, who has, besides willingness to break the rules he knows, a lucky ignorance of the customs of the country. Now, Rossetti was not only almost entirely a foreigner in blood: he was an intruder into painting from poetry. He was Pre-Raphaelite, in Holman Hunt's sense of the term, so far that he was willing, within the limits of his rather rapidly exhausted patience, to be particular and minute, but his motive was quite other than Hunt's or than Ruskin's. For the subject as presented to him by nature he had no respect. He would isolate that in it which appealed to his poetic imagination and he would then surround it with accessories of his own, imported no matter whence, and charged with a significance that the natural, accidental accessories had not possessed. Having no feeling whatever for tone, and a very lively hatred of what he called ' slosh,' he instinctively and deliberately made prominent what painters had long made subsidiary, the pattern. And in pattern he liked the decisive, the recurrent. A great many of his paintings, and more of his drawings, are like sonnets: spaced out in octave and sextet, with visible rhymes at the appointed places. Had he been all that we mean when we say the word painter, we should have had from him greater pictures and drawings, but no such challenge to artistic conventions as was flung out by him.

But there would have been no revolution if Rossetti, Hunt and Millais had not come together while they were still too young to know whither they were, each of them, travelling.

Rossetti, working under Ford Madox Brown and Hunt, certainly had something from both, but he repaid it, to Hunt's advantage rather than Brown's. Look at that most admirable design by Hunt, ' The Lady of Shalott,' in the Tennyson these and other artists illustrated. It is almost wholly Rossetti. But in the genius of Brown, and the most distinctive quality in it, there was something of an honest surliness, a wholesome glowering appreciation of what is knotty, harsh and grotesque in the human comedy. So far as Rossetti and the Pre-Raphaelites reacted on Brown, they drew him, luckily not very far, towards an art in which that had little scope. To put it crudely, with reference to, I suppose, the most famous of Brown's pictures, they made some suggestions towards the adequate, uninspiring Christ Who washes Peter's feet, but the intent, rather irritable, thoroughly characterized Peter was wholly Brown's.

All that, however, was in the future. In 1848 Rossetti, Holman Hunt, Millais, Woolner were very young men, the oldest twenty-three, the youngest nineteen, and they came together at the Royal Academy Schools in a discontent with contemporary painting strong enough to hide from them the unlikelihood of permanent agreement. Hunt and Rossetti were profoundly religious, the one in a very English and Protestant and direct way, the other in a very foreign, sensuous adoration before a veiled beauty. Millais, wonderfully precocious in technique, had no deep thing in him, but was ready then to take Huntsian or Rossettian subjects at the value at which they were proffered, as later on he was willing to take the average Academy subject at the value attached to it by the public. He had no personal scale of values, and neither Hunt's moral respect for the fact nor Rossetti's insolence towards the setting in which it occurred.

All were in some degree literary. Rossetti was already an achieving poet; Woolner was writing, in a sculptor's leisure, ' My Beautiful Lady,' and in 1849 was to project an Arthurian poem, which should occupy him for ' some fifteen years '; Hunt was reading Keats; Millais was trying to write verse; and in the background was Ford Madox Brown, the painter of ' Chaucer,' while Coventry Patmore impinged on the circle. Keats, Tennyson, Browning were constantly under discussion, and Rossetti was ' reciting lots of Patmore, Browning, Mrs Browning.' It was inevitable that the group should presently seek an outlet in literature.

Meanwhile it had made its protest in painting. In 1849 it had exhibited Hunt's ' Rienzi ' and Millais' ' Lorenzo and Isabella '; in 1850, the year in which it produced the *Germ*, it was represented by the ' Carpenter's Shop ' of Millais, sold the day before sending in for £350, and his ' Ferdinand and Ariel,' and Hunt's ' Converted British Family Sheltering a Christian Missionary from the Druids,' sold for £150. These prompt sales, the mildness of criticism in 1849, and the declaration of Samuel Carter Hall, Editor of the *Art Journal*, on seeing the first number of the *Germ*, that the Pre-Raphaelites were ' the future great artists of the age and country,' go some way towards correcting the impression that the Pre-Raphaelites were instantly and uncompromisingly assailed where they were not ignored. To be sure, there was a period of bitter persecution, but

No. 1. *(Price One Shilling.)* JANUARY, 1850.

With an Etching by W. HOLMAN HUNT.

The Germ:

Thoughts towards Nature

In Poetry, Literature, and Art.

When whoso merely hath a little thought
  Will plainly think the thought which is in him,—
  Not imaging another's bright or dim,
Not mangling with new words what others taught;
When whoso speaks, from having either sought
  Or only found,—will speak, not just to skim
  A shallow surface with words made and trim,
But in that very speech the matter brought:
Be not too keen to cry—" So this is all!—
  A thing I might myself have thought as well,
  But would not say it, for it was not worth!"
  Ask: " Is this truth?" For is it still to tell
That, be the theme a point or the whole earth,
Truth is a circle, perfect, great or small?

London:

AYLOTT & JONES, 8, PATERNOSTER ROW.

G. F. TUPPER, Printer, Clement's Lane, Lombard Street.

by 1851 they had their champion in Ruskin, and by 1853, the year of Millais's triumph, they had in some sort prevailed over their enemies. On Rossetti alone was the persecution permanent in effect. The attacks on the ' Ecce Ancilla Domini,' the ' blessed white eyesore ' of his own later condemnation, turned him from directly religious subjects, caused him also to withdraw from public exhibition of his work.

That the *Germ* itself did very much for the Pre-Raphaelites is not to be believed. The challenge thrown out by the group, and after a while taken up by the spokesmen of the established order, was in graphic art, and it cannot be pretended that the four specimens of their art, in a medium the least congenial to them, were as provocative as the paintings they executed in the same year. The importance of the *Germ* lies mainly in the revelation of Dante Gabriel and Christina Rossetti as poets, and poets already arrived at something like maturity. To a certain extent also, though this has not always been observed, the prose in the *Germ* has importance as foreshadowing developments then nearly twenty years in the future. I do not speak of the reviews contributed by William Michael Rossetti. They have some merit as well as some historical interest; and here it may be added that the industry of William Michael as editor of Moxon's Poets and as, from 1850, art critic of the *Spectator*, was quietly useful to the movement. He had perhaps no very sure instinct for the *vraie vérité*, he suffered an element of commonplace to invade his writing, he went too far in emendation of the text of Shelley, he became in old age rather tiresomely garrulous in print about his family, but, for all that, he had genuine and independent appreciation of many things in poetry and art not readily appreciable in 1850, and his educative work was carried on with a mixture of firmness and conciliatoriness that made it really helpful. But, as I have said, it is not of his prose I am thinking: rather, of his brother's. For in certain sentences in the story Dante Gabriel printed in the

Germ we have the earliest of the hints, the later coming from Swinburne's long subsequent essay on drawings by Old Masters at Florence, on which Walter Pater fashioned his style. Who, having quoted to him such a sentence as ' He would feel faint in sunsets and at the sight of stately persons,' but would hesitate over its authorship?

If in the foundation of the Pre-Raphaelite Brotherhood D. G. Rossetti had taken a part less important than those of Hunt and Millais, he was foremost in initiating the *Germ*. In July, 1849, he and his brother and Woolner were trying to arrange with or through William North, author of *Anti-Coningsby*, for ' a monthly sixpenny magazine for which four or five of us would write and one make an etching, each subscribing a guinea and thus becoming a proprietor.' Out of discussion of this project came the *Germ*, the title being chosen out of some sixty suggested, of which the *Seed* had been for a time most favoured. Publishers were found in Messrs Aylott and Jones; printers in Messrs Tupper and Sons; and on, or immediately after, New Year's Day, 1850, there were issued the 700 copies of the first number of *The Germ :/Thoughts towards Nature/In Poetry, Literature, and Art*. Some 400 copies were sold, though not more than 200 to the general public. The net cost of producing this number had been only £18 2s 6d, but after taking sales revenue into account the Pre-Raphaelite Brotherhood had to contribute thirty-five shillings each to meet the deficit, and their distress was piteous. Of the second number they caused only 500 to be printed; the sales were worse; and the magazine was about to come to an end when the printers, as represented by George Tupper, undertook to bear the risk of two more issues, which appeared with the altered title, *Art and Poetry, being Thoughts towards Nature, conducted principally by Artists*, Messrs Dickinson becoming joint publishers.

With the close of the year publication ceased; after 1852 D. G. Rossetti and Millais ceased to be intimate; and next year Millais

Etching for 'The Germ'

HOLMAN HUNT

was an A.R.A., and Hunt, with a religious motive certainly, but perhaps influenced also by thought of what Lewis had discovered there, was looking to the East. Collinson had resigned earlier on religious grounds; Woolner had left for Australia. ' So now the whole Round Table is dissolved,' Dante Gabriel had written to Christina on the election of Millais to the Royal Academy; and she celebrated its dissolution in not too mournful an epicede:

> The P.R.B. is in its decadence:
> For Woolner in Australia cooks his chops:
> And Hunt is yearning for the land of Cheops;
> D. G. Rossetti shuns the vulgar optic;
> While William M. Rossetti merely lops
> His B's in English disesteemed as Coptic.
> Calm Stephens in the twilight smokes his pipe,
> But long the opening of his public day;
> And he at last the champion great Millais,
> Attaining Academic opulence,
> Winds up his signature with A.R.A.
> So rivers merge in the perpetual sea;
> So luscious fruit must fall when over-ripe!
> And so the consummated P.R.B.

Public use of the title P.R.B. had in fact been abandoned before this, as needlessly irritant; and when in December, 1849, Rossetti, Holman Hunt and Stephens had looked over the house in Cheyne Walk in which Rossetti was eventually to live from 1862, they had already been so nervous about the title as to think only half jestingly of inscribing it on the door where it might be explained away as: Please Ring the Bell.

The *Germ*, despite the four etchings, the expository articles by G. F. Stephens and Ford Madox Brown, and the declaration on the back of its first number that it would in art ' encourage and enforce an entire adherence to the simplicity of nature,' was much more successful in presenting the new poetry than in illustrating and defending the new art.

To review its contents: the first number had for frontispiece an etching in two compartments by Holman Hunt, not unworthy of him in conception, but vitiated by his incapacity to give his characteristic detail in that medium. Opposite to it was the beginning of Woolner's poem, ' My Beautiful Lady,' followed by ' Of My Lady in Death,' pieces eventually shaped into his volume of 1863. These compositions have numerous weaknesses, sometimes those common in amateur verse, occasionally resultant from a Leigh Huntsian misuse of words, as in ' my head sank on her bosom's heave '; and, as Coventry Patmore had acutely noted when he heard them in 1849, ' each stanza stands too much alone, and has its own ideas too much to itself.' But, for all that, they possess a certain sculptural quality then unusual enough to excite comment. After them came a sonnet by Ford Madox Brown, of no account as poetry, yet with its small contribution to the painter's way of looking at the world in the phrase ' line-blending twilight.'

Theory came in with a rather ingenious essay by J. L. Tupper on ' The Subject in Art,' insisting that subjects in painting affect the beholder precisely as if he came on them in nature, and pleading for more attention to contemporary subjects, but really amusing only in the argument that whereas a pheasant at the poulterer's is a bird, on a canvas it is food.

But it was the poetry that made the first number of the *Germ* a great event, and its poetry, in the full sense, begins with Coventry Patmore's stanzas, in their own kind unsurpassed in his later work, ' The Seasons ':

> The crocus, in the shrewd March morn,
> Thrusts up his saffron spear;
> And April dots the sombre thorn
> With gems, and loveliest cheer.

Then sleep the seasons, full of might;
While slowly swells the pod,
And rounds the peach, and in the night
The mushroom bursts the sod.

The winter comes: the frozen rut
Is bound with silver bars;
The white drift heaps against the hut;
And night is pierced with stars.

On the reverse of the page holding that is Christina Rossetti's
'Dream Land,' not quite the earliest published of her lyrics, since
two short pieces by her had appeared in the *Athenæum* in 1848, but
the first to give her characteristic note:

Rest, rest, for evermore
Upon a mossy shore,
Rest, rest, that shall endure
Till time shall cease;
Sleep that no pain shall wake,
Night that no morn shall break,
Till joy shall overtake
Her perfect peace.

There we are almost within sight of the Swinburne of 'The Garden
of Proserpine.'

Facing this poem of Christina's is Dante Gabriel's very early and
not wholly personal 'My Sister's Sleep,' announced by the title in
the *Germ* as No. 1 of 'Songs of One Household,' but certainly alone
in his work. The *Germ* had it by accident; or, to speak more piously,
the most high Muses contrived to keep the editress of the *Belle
Assemblée*, who had admired it enthusiastically, from using it in her
unworthy pages. Dante Gabriel came to dislike it, and when in 1869
he was collecting his verse for the famous volume of the next year
he included it only at the urging of Swinburne and other advisers,

and only after deleting the weak seventh, eighth, twelfth and thirteenth stanzas. As indicative of the poor matter then excised, I
quote the two stanzas which, in the *Germ*, followed the sixth of the
final text:

> Silence was speaking at my side
> With an exceedingly clear voice:
> I knew the calm as of a choice
> Made in God for me, to abide.
>
> I said, ' Full knowledge does not grieve:
> This which upon my spirit dwells
> Perhaps would have been sorrow else:
> But I am glad 'tis Christmas Eve.'

Dante Gabriel's youth when he composed it, the influence of the
earlier Coventry Patmore, possibly too some hint from Hood, may
explain the simplicity and domestic sentiment of some lines of the
poem, but it is so far in accord with the ideals of the Pre-Raphaelites
that it educes spiritual significance out of its well-observed details,
and already there is a rare subtlety in rendering certain sensations,
with something of that grave expectancy which was to cause Walter
Pater to regard Rossetti as a poet for whom every moment was a
crisis.

Dante Gabriel's contributions in verse, like his sister's, were
pieces written before the *Germ* had been even dimly projected;
his solitary contribution in prose was deliberately written for the
first number of the periodical. ' Hand and Soul,' often as it has been
praised, has hardly had full recognition for the astonishing originality and assurance of its prose. That a man of twenty-one, un-
exercised in prose, incurious about the work of the masters of that
' other harmony,' without any model—for the obligation to the
Stories After Nature of Charles Wells cannot be taken seriously—
should produce, at his first attempt, prose so distinctive and un-

Etching for 'The Germ'

W. H. DEVERELL

fumbling is really more wonderful than that he should write in youth such a poem as ' The Blessed Damozel.' There is no occasion to look about for passages of special eloquence. The opening sentences, with their unobtrusive but very definite idiosyncrasy, will suffice to remind us of the quality of this confident novice's prose:

Before any knowledge of painting was brought to Florence, there were already painters in Lucca, and Pisa, and Arezzo who feared God and loved the art. The keen, grave workmen from Greece, whose trade it was to sell their own works in Italy and teach Italians to imitate them, had already found rivals of the soil with skill that would forestall their lessons and cheapen their crucifixes and *addolorate*, more years than is supposed before the art came at all into Florence. The pre-eminence to which Cimabue was raised at once by his contemporaries, and which he still retains to a wide extent even in the modern mind, is to be accounted for, partly by the circumstances under which he arose, and partly by that extraordinary *purpose of fortune* born with the lives of some few, and through which it is not a little thing for any who went before if they are even remembered as the shadows of the coming of such an one, and the voices which prepared his way in the wilderness. It is thus, almost exclusively, that the painters of whom I speak are now known. They have left little, and but little heed is taken of that which men hold to have been surpassed; it is gone like time gone—a track of dust and dead leaves that merely led to the fountain.

There is a paragraph of not obviously heightened prose which, doing its introductory business perfectly, does so much more than its immediate business. And then there is the plausibility of the unlaboured evidence, enviable by any professed writer of fiction, the mythical Dr Amemster called in to testify to the quality of the work of the invented Chiaro dell' Erma, the cited exemplar of that painter's work. But for us here what matters most is that ' Hand and Soul,' more than anything else between the wrappers of the *Germ*, suggests the spiritual ideals of the movement, giving to Pre-Raphaelitism a more intimate meaning than it had in the penitential and yet largely exterior thought of Holman Hunt, the sponge-like, absorbing and presently-to-be-squeezed-out mind of Millais.

In the first number of the *Germ*, at Woolner's instance, the names of authors had not been given; in the second, though Christina Rossetti screened herself behind the pseudonym ' Ellen Alleyn,' and F. G. Stephens behind ' John Seward,' the identity of contributors was generally revealed.

The second number opened with a piece, in rather feeble blank verse, by James Collinson, its subject ' The Child Jesus,' faced by his not very impressive etching in illustration of it. On this followed ' A Pause of Thought,' written by Christina Rossetti two years earlier, when she was only seventeen, and showing how early she was consciously seeking poetic fame and ' sick of hope deferred.' The next item, an article by Stephens on ' The Purpose and Tendency of Early Italian Art,' records with admiration that in English landscape there had been ' an entire seeking after originality in a more humble manner than has been practised since the decline of Italian Art,' only to urge English ' historical painters ' to follow that example. ' Historical ' painting receives further attention, in a brief, practical essay, never continued, by Ford Madox Brown. Christina Rossetti reappears with a song, ' Oh! roses for the flush of youth.' Other poems in this number are ' Morning Sleep,' a piece of some length by William Bell Scott, reprinted, with modifications, in his *Poems* of 1875, and ' Stars and Moon ' by Coventry Patmore, in that somewhat sententious second-best manner of his. These last two contributions associate with the *Germ* men who were never of the inner group, and who fell away from it, Patmore comparatively soon, Scott at long last in circumstances of posthumous scandal.

As I shall not return to Scott, I may say here that the final

Etching for 'The Germ'

JAMES COLLINSON

criticism of him exists not in any prose estimate but in the generous yet frank elegy written by Swinburne. When William Minto, who had been in touch with several members of the circle, gave the world the autobiographical notebooks of Scott, with their jealous and occasionally very offensive references to his betters, Swinburne hastened to dub Scott dauber and rhymer; but the earlier tribute remains. Strenuous, unachieving, Scott, if hardly deserving of study, remains above contempt.

To continue with an enumeration of the contents of the two subsequent numbers of the *Germ* is unnecessary. W. M. Rossetti remained titular editor, but felt obliged to acquiesce in whatever was proposed to him by the Tuppers, and in consequence, together with matter by the original contributors, these numbers contained work by John and George Tupper, written, it would seem, for the ribald student public they valued, but disconcerting to readers who had had ' The Blessed Damozel ' and ' Dream Land.'

IV

As an exhibition of certain novel and beautiful things, in poetry rather than in graphic art, the *Germ* was and remains important; but it had neither a consistent fighting policy, such as only a professional literary journalist could have given it, nor funds, and its circulation was much too small, its life much too short, for it to affect more than a minute section of the public. But in any event its principal contributors were coming before the public in another place, in the Royal Academy, and it was over the new painting rather than over the new poetry that, for some years, the battle was to be fought.

Familiar as the facts are, it seems that few critics of Victorian literature have understood, or at least duly emphasized, the tardiness with which that new poetry, so clearly announced in the *Germ*, came before the general body of readers. It is essential, if we would see Rossetti and his associates with the eyes of their contemporaries, to bear in mind that for the public, so far as it was made aware of them, they were from, say, 1850 to well after 1860 simply innovatory painters, not workers at once in literature and pictorial art. The first wonderful volume of the poetry of William Morris, the translations of early Italian poets issued by Rossetti, the highly remarkable ' Queen Mother and Rosamund ' of Swinburne, all work published some years later than the date at which we have arrived, were books which fell dead on appearance. Only Christina Rossetti's initial volume awoke any response. ' She,' Swinburne always insisted, ' was our Jael.'

Matters might have gone very differently. To be sure, Swinburne,

Etching for 'The Germ'
HOLMAN HUNT

the youngest of the group, and a poet who, as I have been at pains to show in my *Study of Swinburne*, was slow to discover, or at least to indulge, his exuberant lyrical genius, could have published no volume of miscellaneous lyrical work before 1863. But had Dante Gabriel Rossetti, Christina Rossetti and William Morris united to issue in the 'fifties a small joint volume of poems, their combined appeal could hardly have lacked considerable answer; and the new painting was most easily approachable, was in fact later on most commonly approached with sympathy, through the new poetry.

Whether as painters or as poets, Rossetti and his associates demanded of intending students a rich, carefully discriminated æsthetic experience. A good deal of their work could not be apprehended without initiation, and the agencies for such initiation were to seek. They suffered from lack of an indirectly educative Press for one thing, even more than, a generation later, the little men of the 'nineties suffered from a criticism too well prepared to receive them. But, undeniably, that they should have been dependent in that way, that they should not have been directly apprehensible, argues that, in at least part of their work, they were of the secondary order of artists. In the work of their weaker moments, and in the work of their disciples, it is impossible not to feel that there is some exploitation of what is conventionally ' poetical,' even though the convention be novel. Their difficulty, in those weaker moments, the difficulty of their disciples, may perhaps be best likened to that which has been experienced by certain symbolists, even by so rare and scrupulous a poet as Mr Yeats. The symbol, so finely significant when the poet's imagination first produced it, tends to be used again and again, in an unconscious indolence of the imagination, when a new symbol, exactly appropriate to the new poem, should be fashioned by a fresh energy. With Rossetti's group, and still more with its disciples, we find from time to time a reliance on exotic, antique, mystical accessories, which are used with an unjustified confidence that their mere presence in the picture or poem will give it high artistic value. Those accessories, to be sure, are exquisite; they are incomparably more valuable than the properties used by the academic painters of 1850 or in such professedly romantic poetry as Sir Walter Scott's; but, fundamentally, that confidence has no more justification than the academic painter's belief in the power of Mary Queen of Scots to give tragic significance to any competently done picture of her execution. It was one of Rossetti's greatest services to the movement that, himself not infallible, he insisted with so much force on the necessity of a constant renewal of the energy by which the artist finds the new means for the new task. Very dangerous to disciples who did not fully understand him, he at least was usually vigilant in the perils of his method.

Dante Gabriel Rossetti's is a poetry almost too concrete, often grotesquely anthropocentric, and it is a poetry without relief. A dreamer, to whom dreams came with the solidity and definition of waking life, and whose every dream was heavily charged with significance, he seemed almost always under one or other of those mysterious compulsions which are imposed upon the somnambulist, hardly ever free, certainly never irresponsible. This, though they find cruder words for it, is what people have in mind when they complain of the oppressiveness of his work as a poet. It is oppressive. The oppression begins with the metrical form, always fine, of a poet never metrically spontaneous as his great sister almost invariably was. Metres come to Swinburne with the pulses throbbing in his head, intoxicate him, sweep him on to his best things and his worst, delight him so much that he cannot always desist when his subject has been expressed. Nothing of the sort ever happens with Rossetti. There is a rich and sustained music in every sonnet, line after line ' of its own arduous fulness reverent,' but the music is an accompaniment, strictly subordinated to the intellectual structure and emotional development and pictorial effects of the poem, not itself an inspiration. Indeed, I can think of only one passage in Rossetti in which music has been allowed to have its uncontrolled way, but that is among the loveliest he wrote:

> Poets' fancies all are there:
> There the elf-girls flood with wings
> Valleys full of plaintive air;
> There breathe perfumes; there in rings
> Whirl the foam-bewildered springs;
> Siren there
> Winds her dizzy hair and sings.

And to the metrical oppression is added that resulting from his refusal to admit into his House of Life anything which has not an intimate association. He will not allow himself or his reader the relief of indifferent things in that House which is a reliquary. Nor, in admitting Nature, will he yield to her, content that the sun and the sea should lighten his verse and reverberate in it with as much or as little meaning as they have for us in our common experience of them. The phenomena of Nature are admitted by him only on condition that they enter his verse with a very personal significance, reduced to symbols.

33

V

AFTER Rossetti and the *Germ*, William Morris and the *Oxford and Cambridge Magazine*.

The *Oxford and Cambridge*, published by Bell and Daldy, was financially the responsibility of Morris, though Richard Watson Dixon was anxious to afford what help he could out of his small means; and, if the three numbers to which Rossetti contributed be left out of account, it was Morris who gave it literary importance. All the same, the share Morris had in it can be exaggerated. Before the appearance of the second number, February, 1856, editorial control was transferred to Fulford, who had a salary of £100 a year, for the year the magazine lived. As for the contents, like those of every professedly artistic periodical issued in England, with the solitary exception of the *Savoy* in the 'nineties, they were too miscellaneous to point in any particular direction. Vernon and Godfrey Lushington; the sociological and political journalist Bernard Cracroft: I do not know, and am but languidly moved to ask, what they were doing in the company of Morris and Rossetti.

Rossetti gave the magazine three highly characteristic poems: ' Nineveh,' intellectually, I suppose, the greatest thing he ever did, for the August number; the already printed ' Blessed Damozel,' for November; ' The Staff and the Scrip,' for December. Morris, a contributor to ten out of the twelve numbers, wrote for it eight prose stories, five poems, an article on Amiens cathedral, an article on certain engravings by Alfred Rethel, and in an all but unique condescension to reviewing, certainly the only review he undertook willingly, a notice of Browning's ' Men and Women.' One poem,

34

No. I.   JANUARY, 1856.   PRICE 1s.

THE

Oxford & Cambridge Magazine,

CONDUCTED BY MEMBERS OF THE

TWO UNIVERSITIES.

CONTENTS.

LONDON:
BELL AND DALDY, FLEET STREET.

PRINTED BY C. WHITTINGHAM,   TOOKS COURT, CHANCERY LANE.

' Winter Weather,' was left in the files; the others were included in *The Defence of Guenevere*, issued two years later. The prose stories Morris persistently undervalued.

One of those tales, certainly, is of little worth. 'Frank's Sealed Letter,' an excursion into the modern world, has, however, its interest as evidence to the truth that near things were as remote to its author as remote things were near. For Morris was never more archaic, in the unhappy sense, than in this awkward approach to contemporary life, the things he had seen with physical eyes receding from him into an odd, dim, distant world. But the other tales, if they have not the perfection of the late romances, have the peculiar charm of young work, the dew still on the just discovered roses. In the world of Morris it is never noon, with its challenge to the artist to render full illumination, but always either morning or evening, with a sun the rays of which can be rendered in a convention applicable only to sunrise and sunset, with an atmosphere of hopeful adventurousness, the chances of the day before one, or of a luxuriously and wholesomely achieved retrospect, and with the values that colours have as they emerge from grey or are about to disappear into darkness. The oblique rays here are those of morning.

Even lovelier than the prose, which for good and evil has not yet been thoroughly conventionalized, is the inset verse. There are not ten things even in our mystery-haunted poetry to set beside the miraculous song of Margaret in ' The Hollow Land ':

Christ keep the Hollow Land
All the summer-tide;
Still we cannot understand
Where the waters glide;

Only dimly seeing them
Coldly slipping through
Many green-lipp'd cavern mouths
Where the hills are blue.

VI

THE world of William Morris, taken as a whole, is the sanest and most happily ordered that any modern English writer has made. 'How I love the earth and the seasons and weather, and all things that deal with them, and all that grows out of them,' he wrote: no one has loved these things in so complete a contentment with just what they are, without romantical fuss over them; no one has been so happy in appreciating the succession of the seasons and the propriety of what each brings with it.

> Many scarlet bricks there were
> In its walls, and old grey stone;
> Over which red apples shone
> At the right time of the year.

'At the right time of the year': if ever a single word gave us a poet's attitude towards the world, the epithet 'right' gives us the attitude of Morris. But here, in the volume from which I quote, *The Defence of Guenevere*, as nowhere else in Morris, there is at times a strange distortion of natural things, the trees of the conventional landscape twisted by an evil wind, the hills heaped up and dwindled as in a brain-sick traveller's changing fancies, almost all things brought too near or removed to a terrifying distance, the very sun swung out of its course and the moon become a menace. Those fierce and convulsive poems, 'The Defence' itself and 'Arthur's Tomb,' are the work of one who was to be the writer of the most equably and naturally flowing narrative that we have, and their movement is widdershins, and the words come to us in gasps.

Cartoon

D. G. ROSSETTI

(including portraits of Swinburne and Christina Rossetti)

Take the great passages in ' The Defence '; and first the presentation by the queen to her accusers of the parable of the cloths of Heaven and Hell. It is what Pater was to call Browning's, ' a poetry of situations,' and no doubt in that respect produced under the influence of Browning, but with how much originality, all the same!

> Listen, suppose your time were come to die,
> And you were quite alone and very weak;
> Yea, laid a dying while very mightily
>
> The wind was ruffling up the narrow streak
> Of river through your broad lands running well:
> Suppose a hush should come, then someone speak:
>
> ' One of these cloths is heaven, and one is hell,
> Now choose one cloth for ever, which they be,
> I will not tell you, you must somehow tell . . .'
>
> After a shivering half-hour you said,
> ' God help! heaven's colour, the blue '; and he said, ' hell.'
> Perhaps you then would roll upon your bed,
>
> And cry to all good men that loved you well,
> ' Ah Christ! if only I had known, known, known ';
> Lancelot went away, then I could tell,
>
> Like wisest man, how all things would be, moan,
> And roll and hurt myself, and long to die,
> And yet fear much to die for what was sown.

There was hardly an intelligent contemporary writer of verse who could not have managed the transitions better than they are managed in this poem and in ' Arthur's Tomb '; there was not one capable of quite Morris's fierce hold on situation. The very defects have a kind of merit, in speeches of stammering or hysterical passion, as when Guinevere breaks into the purely feminine, in itself inadequate, in its context so effective, outcry—' O bad! bad! ' And, at the greatest height reached in these poems, there is the utterance of Guenevere wounding herself in wounding Lancelot with such edged and poisoned words as these:

Banner of Arthur—with black-bended shield

Sinister-wise across the fair gold ground
Here let me tell you what a knight you are,
O sword and shield of Arthur! you are found
A crooked sword, I think, that leaves a scar

On the bearer's arm, so be he thinks it straight,
Twisted Malay's crease beautiful blue-grey,
Poison'd with sweet fruit; as he found too late,
My husband Arthur, on some bitter day!

O sickle cutting hemlock the day long!
That the husbandman across his shoulder hangs,
And, going homeward about evensong,
Dies the next morning, struck through by the fangs!

In these things, and less spasmodically in ' Sir Peter Harpdon's End ' and ' The Haystack in the Floods,' there is the one quality of great poetry which the later work of Morris, so much more finished, lacked: the quality of intensity. Something went out of his poetry with the passing of not many years, as something went out of Rossetti's, out of Swinburne's.

In Rossetti's case and in Swinburne's, partial explanations, to my mind of little value, can be found in physical causes and in circumstances, and there are those who may be content to say ' chloral ' or ' Putney.' But perhaps this new poetry had on it some doom, was not related quite closely enough to what in life is inexhaustible material for the artist, was the poetry of men who could not profit as artists by the whole of their experience. Here it becomes necessary to be careful, for with a good deal, especially at first, in common these poets have very definite individualities, and it is quite certain that neither with them nor with any other group, school, or movement shall we find identity of aim, as with men banded together for some political or other exterior purpose.

Rossetti's exclusion of so much of himself from his poetry is far from being without parallel: most poets have chosen to express but a small part of themselves, and it is at the cost of his poetry that an exception, Wordsworth, puts the whole of himself into verse. But Rossetti's choice, wise certainly in itself, is perhaps on a broad view of poetry too fastidious a rejection of material not evidently to the poet's purpose. The poet, to be sure, must admit into his verse nothing that is not poetry, but after all it is for transmutation of base metal that we praise the alchemist. One insinuates so much under rebuke by a memory of ' Jenny,' and acknowledging that, since not everything can be done with any one instrument, Rossetti was in the main right to limit himself; the point is merely that the poet was so much more limited than the man. Morris, who made the production of poetry seem more natural than any other poet of our time has made it, also eventually made it seem incidental, one activity out of many, not more important than weaving at the loom or any other craftsman's labour. But the greatest poetry is the sublime summary of the poet's whole experience. With Swinburne, who gave himself completely to poetry, there was hope that it would be; and, indeed, in one volume, his best, it is. That volume, *Songs Before Sunrise*, in just eulogy of which he said ' my other books are books, it is myself,' gives us Swinburne in vividly realized relationship to the prime energies of nature and most permanent passions of mankind. But, on the whole, and especially after 1880, Swinburne was too much a song to be a singer, poetry having ceased to be his achievement in becoming his existence, so that, among other consequences, a prosodist's praise of his later technique may irritate us like a physiologist's praise of the technique of a man breathing.

In one way or another, these poets seem destined to a less satisfying or less enduring relationship between their poetry and normal human experience than we find in most of the very greatest. Perhaps it is the destiny of Romanticism, the price it must pay for its peculiar successes, more valuable to the modern spirit, certainly, than classic successes, that it should be in some such precarious relationship. Or, to speak more carefully, perhaps it is the destiny of a thoroughly conscious Romanticism.

VII

It is in an increasingly conscious allegiance to its ideal that the poetry of the Romantics differs from that of their predecessors. The romantic element is everywhere in English poetry. Ostensibly excluded in the eighteenth century, after the magnificent excesses of the Elizabethan age and the 'fair and flagrant things' which delighted the poets of the next generation, it creeps in, not only with Collins and Dyer and the Thomson of certain passages, but with the condemning phrases of its enemies, unsuspected, as in Johnson's protest against those who would 'number the streaks of the tulip,' and in Pope's mocking

> Die of a rose in aromatic pain.

Johnson himself exemplifies, for all his outer John Bullishness, that 'hunger of the imagination which preys on life,' and anticipates Rossetti's admirable requirement that poetry should be 'amusing' in praising *Coriolanus* as 'one of the most amusing of our author's performances.' It is not a new thing that the Romantics, from Blake and Coleridge onwards, bring into English poetry; it is a new consciousness of its importance. With the Victorian Romantics that consciousness has become acute, to their gain and their peril.

It is a question whether the error of those who would serve beauty with too exclusive and purposed an art is not almost as serious as that of those who would use art for the direct magnification of God. In Rossetti, at any rate, only not in 'Jenny' and 'Nineveh' and some four or five other pieces, there is a concentration on the purely æsthetic effect which, in a kind of search for short cuts to beauty, has its dangers, as the view of life taken at one period by William Morris, his human figures appearing to be worked on tapestry against a world that is just so much *décor*, has others. But we need not suppose either Morris or Rossetti ignorant of the perils and limitations of æsthetic and conventionalized poetry. A well-known criticism by Morris of Swinburne, betraying misapprehension of its immediate subject, shows him well aware of the importance of full life in poetry. And as for Rossetti, after Coleridge the least fallible of all English poets in treatment of the principles of art, I need cite only a certain letter of his, dated 1855, to William Allingham. He is censuring a piece by his friend because it ' chiefly awakens contemplation, like a walk on a fine day with a churchyard in it,' whereas it should rouse one ' like a part of one's own life,' and leave one ' to walk it off as one might live it off.'

VIII

THE capital truth about William Morris was stated in that passage of Mr Mackail's admirable biography in which, admitting that Morris never worked as an architect, he said that it was always in the spirit of the architect that Morris worked. Unique in the modern world, William Morris worked always from the centre, caring little what portion of the circumference he struck in his energetic excursions. In a sense, and of course, he was an amateur. What else could a man be who was poet, designer, printer, and, in the overflow of his vitality, reformer of economic and social conditions? In each department, the expert may question the legitimacy of his success. Those Kelmscott publications, are they in the central tradition of great printing? That typography, that decoration, do they not get rather too much between the reader and the thing to be conveyed to him? In regard to poetry, especially, since the mere writing down of it is a materialization which the absolute lover of poetry must resent, is not that way of conveying, say, Chaucer to us the result of a misconception of his need and ours? Should a wallpaper, which will be a background for pictures, be a thing so nearly competitive with them?

For myself, I think Whistler's book, *The Gentle Art of Making Enemies*, a more precise and scrupulous adjustment of means to ends than any publication for which Morris was responsible, and I do not doubt that Whistler had generally a juster feeling for the limits within which decoration is lawful. But Whistler remains for the most part, only not in the portraits of his mother and of Carlyle, the butterfly of his signature, and Morris was very much a man.

45

Whistler, with the whole science of each of his instruments, is never an amateur: no, not even, though Mr Max Beerbohm has urged the contrary, in his prose. Whistler is an expert who happens to be a specialist in several mediums. He gets his effects unerringly, by an exquisite care in choosing out of the gross profusion of life what is to his purpose, but also by narrowing that purpose till his work, the two supreme portraits and a very few other things apart, becomes very slight. Morris, with a more obvious convention, has an immensely wider purpose. He is alone among the artists of the group in this, that instead of drawing in to his centre, he strikes out from it in every direction.

If there was any development in Morris, it was in his poetry, and it was not altogether fortunate. He began by recreating, in that wonderful first volume *The Defence of Guenevere*, the life of the Middle Ages, apprehended with faultless intuition, but from without. He proceeded by allowing himself to be drawn into the Middle Ages, as if Columbus should dwindle into a colonist, forgetting the excitement of discovery. It is not exactly a poet who addresses us in *The Earthly Paradise*, rather a worker of tapestry who has taken verse for his medium. The craftsmanship is, in its sort, perfect, with an instinctive subdual of the separate line lest it should stand out excessively in the pattern. But this is not, in the full sense, creation; it is the leisurely, unemphatic display of figures no more real than those on tapestry. With the Norse influence there is a return to creation. There is no more the effect of stories told by aged, wearied men who would value them rather for the equable flow of narrative than for any pungency of characterization or intensity of emotion. Something larger and looser and much more nearly epic has come into the verse, which, all the same, has neither the clairvoyance nor the edge of the first great immature volume, and in which there is no trace of the wizardry of three or four of the strangest early poems. Apart from these works, there are the late lyrics, undervalued as it seems to me, with their peculiar beauty in the treatment of gracious, homely things, and a kind of unexcited appreciation of the tenderness of human affections to which there is no parallel, and there are those prose romances, the most purely happy books in modern English literature, reaching back into the past or anticipating a fortunate future. But nowhere is there the perfected work of that poet who was announced in the *Defence of Guenevere* volume.

Outside the arts, there is that development which turned the idle singer of an empty day into an active Socialist; but there is nothing more in all that than the discovery of hostility between the modern factory-dominated world and the conditions of joyous and efficient artistic production. Morris has become aware of another portion of the circumference, and strikes out at it, but it is from the same centre that he issues, burly and choleric and benevolent, to do the job that had escaped attention. With a good head, and a good heart, and good hands, a man could do anything that needed doing. He was highly capable, in a hurry, and short-tempered with the secrets of the several arts and with economics. He took things in his stride, and got back to his centre, ready for the next day's work, in whatever direction it might lie, and made no fuss about what he had done or would do. Various as his achievements were, they were very decidedly one man's, and it was so that he worked, like the ship's captain that he looked, or a farmer, or an all-round craftsman. The pedantry of applying specialized æsthetic measuring instruments to what he did in so many departments is rebuked by the personality of so great, simple, hasty and universal a creature. To judge him by what he did in any one matter is like judging a man's life by what he does on Mondays.

IX

THE relation of Coventry Patmore, never admitted by himself, to what four years later was to be called Pre-Raphaelitism was acutely perceived in 1844 by Bulwer Lytton. Patmore's early verse had been received in some quarters with abuse. Thus a reviewer in *Blackwood*, shrewd enough to suspect that the younger generation of poets were drawing on Keats and Shelley, had cried out on the appearance of Patmore's volume, ' This is the life into which the slime of the Keateses (*sic*) and Shelleys of former times has fecundated.' But Bulwer Lytton, in a queerly phrased, oddly punctuated, intelligently discriminating letter to the young poet, put his finger on almost every virtue and defect, deprecating the intrusion of prose matter, warning him against excessive particularity: ' It seems to me that, in common with Tennyson, you cultivate details to the injury of the broad whole.'

Patmore was already, in his own way, practising Pre-Raphaelitism. Brought into contact with the group, through Woolner, in 1849, and drawn more especially towards Holman Hunt, he remained intimate with most of its members till 1853. They applauded his often repeated, ' It is the last rub that polishes the mirror '; they were impressed by his blunt declaration that even Tennyson's best work was ' not finished *from within*.' For a while he was to several of them that most useful counsellor who is at once sympathetic and detached. But for the accident of Patmore's prolonged absence from London after the death of his first wife, he might have maintained with D. G. Rossetti the friendship he tried too late to revive. But his relation was to Pre-Raphaelitism proper, not to that development

48

in which Rossetti, Morris, Burne-Jones, and in a way Swinburne, were the dominating figures. His affinity was with the early Holman Hunt, and with the Millais of 'The Woodman's Daughter,' a subject taken from his poems. Realistic, with a purpose far other than the usual realist's, and destined to become the celebrant of that supreme mystery of God's love for the soul of man, Patmore was not for long moving on lines parallel to those on which his friends advanced.

X

SEBASTIAN EVANS, who was two years younger than Rossetti, and outlived Swinburne by two years, was never of Rossetti's circle, but in later life was intimate with Burne-Jones, and in his passion for the medieval and in the ease with which he turned from poetry to applied art had a good deal in common with William Morris. Member of a family which in three generations showed exceptional versatility, he was perhaps predestined to dissipate his energy in too many directions, yet there seems to be some personal capriciousness in his repeated transfer of devotion from painting, wood-carving, and designing for a glass factory to journalism, political agitation, legal work; poetry and antiquarian research seldom getting more than his spare hours. No doubt his version of the old French romance of Perceval, *The High History of the Holy Graal*, and his study of the legend, *In Quest of the Holy Graal*, count for more than his poems, most of the best of which were contained in *Brother Fabian's Manuscript*, 1865. But the blend of Pre-Raphaelite colour with an individual humour gives many of his poems distinction. After Richard Watson Dixon, with whom he had also a less technical affinity, he is perhaps the most successful Victorian user of *terza rima*; and *Dudman in Paradise* is a curiously fortunate blend of reverence and mockery.

His sister Anne, who was born in 1820 and died in 1870, had probably more talent for music than for poetry. At least, she found comfort in ' the tangible restraints ' of its laws, whereas ' the more indefinite freedom ' of painting and poetry often, as her brother noted, ' oppressed and alarmed her.' She wrote, however, one piece with a queer, simple magic in it, coming for that moment into the line of succession from the Christina Rossetti of *Goblin Market* to the Mary Coleridge of so many fantasies.

Tirlywirly, all alone,
Spinning under a yew;
Something came with no noise,
But Tirlywirly knew.

Tirlywirly sate spinning,
Never looked around;
Something made a black shadow
Creep on the ground.

Tirlywirly sate spinning,
Spinning fast for fear;
Something spoke a dark word
Close at her ear . . .

XI

THE *Dark Blue*, 1871-1873, founded by John C. Freund in the belief that, independently of any particular group or generation of Oxford undergraduates, there was an Oxford point of view, had no very definite aim. From the first it contained a proportion of commonplace matter, and in its third volume it became merely one of the magazines of its day. Still, its contributors included W. M. Rossetti, Dr Franz Hueffer, H. D. Traill, Andrew Lang, Sir Sidney Colvin, W. H. Mallock, and, much more to our purpose, D. G. Rossetti, Swinburne, Simeon Solomon, Arthur O'Shaughnessy.

Rossetti's contribution was the poem ' Down Stream,' illustrated by almost the only significant drawing published by the *Dark Blue*, a drawing by Ford Madox Brown of a man and a girl embracing in a boat, the girl's full, poetical yet homely face admirably observed in the innocent animalism with which it accepts love. The one other drawing worth looking at is Simeon Solomon's design for the poem by Swinburne, here entitled ' The End of the Month,' but afterwards printed in the second series of *Poems and Ballads* as ' At a Month's End.' It is stated in the *Dictionary of National Biography* that this magnificent poem, the finest of Swinburne's few poems of passion as distinguished from erotic fever, was inspired by Solomon's design; but the design is dated 1871, and the poem, the original manuscript of which I have examined, is almost certainly of earlier date. It is true that Swinburne was sometimes moved to poetry by the pictures of his friends: if he did not get his first inspiration for ' Before the Mirror ' from Whistler's beautiful painting of Jo

May 15. 1871
12 Fitzroy St. W.

My dear Swinburne
            Many thanks for
your kindness. I have just sent
a letter to the Editor of the Dark
Blue telling him of your offer.
and suggesting that it might
be in the June number and as
I know how swiftly you write
I think that would be possible:
would it not? it is today only
the 15th. (I hope I have done nothing in bad taste in thus writing
to the D.B. (O, monsieur) but if I
don't look after myself no-
one will do it for me. I cannot tell you what pleasure it

will give me to all something by
you or me (that sounds rather
improper) and in print. I
suppose the editor will com-
municate with you.

Your letter is delightful and
I could tell you much for on
Friday I was taken by Hunt's
counsel to the Trial – there were
some very funny things said
but nothing improper. except
the disgusting and silly medi-
cal evidence of which I heard
but very little – Reynolds pub-
lishes everything and the D.T.
does nearly the same I think
the public interest has quite

died away. I saw the writer of those highly effusive letters he looks rather humdrum certainly - oddly enough after the morning trial when I left court I was ravenous and went to the nearest restaurant where I found B——n, P——k and H——t at lunch all three solicitors. Knowing the solicitor I sat down with them, which, as it was a public crowded room I had no hesitation in doing, B——n is very remarkable, he is not quite beautiful but extremely pretty, a perfect figure, manner, and voice altogether I was agreeably surprised at him — of course they will be acquitted - it is very hard for Hurt and Fisk to be mixed up with the two others - I am so

glad to be able to relieve your mind
with regard to your first letter.
I _did_ destroy it. but I thought you would
think it a very poor compliment
to do so I did not like telling you
I quite appreciate your story
about the character — I will
write soon again and thanken
you much believe me
      your aff'ly yrs
      S Solomon

Heffernan,[1] he reshaped the piece as a tribute to Whistler, and he wrote ' Cleopatra ' for the drawing by Frederick Sandys. But work of the quality of ' At a Month's End ' is no more likely to be produced while putting words to a picture than while putting words to a tune. There is, however, Swinburne's own authority for the ascription of ' Erotion ' to the influence of a drawing by Solomon. But the more interesting point of contact between Swinburne and the painter is in the poet's long article, in the *Dark Blue* : ' Simeon Solomon: Notes on his " Vision of Love " and other Studies.' Since Swinburne, who came, naturally enough, to despise the character of Solomon, never reprinted the essay, it does not lie to the hand of the ordinary reader, and I may quote a typical passage. Writing of the persons in the pictures of this Hellenist of the Hebrews, he says:

There is a questioning wonder in their faces, a fine joy and a faint sorrow, a trouble as of water stirred, a delight as of thirst appeased. Always, at feast or sacrifice, in chamber or in field, the air and carriage of their beauty has something in it of strange: hardly a figure but has some touch, though never so delicately slight, either of eagerness or of weariness, some note of expectation or of satiety, some semblance of outlook or inlook: but prospective or introspective, an expression is there which is not pure Greek, a shade or tone of thought or feeling beyond Hellenic contemplation; whether it be oriental or modern in its origin, and derive from national or personal sources. This passionate sentiment of mystery seems at times to ' o'erinform its tenement ' of line and colour, and impress itself even to perplexity upon the sense of the spectator.

And he goes on to remark of Solomon's one essay in literature, that ' read by itself as a fragment of spiritual allegory, this written " Vision of Love revealed in Sleep " seems to want even that much

[1] The poem, the original manuscript of which I have examined in Mr. Wise's collection, was developed out of three of the four stanzas of ' A Dreamer,' written in 1862.

coherence which is requisite to keep symbolic or allegorical art from absolute dissolution or collapse.' The complaint is just. 'The Vision of Love revealed in Sleep,' written in 1869 during a visit to Oscar Browning in Rome, privately printed in 1871, enlarged and published in the same year, remains, nevertheless, an amateur effort in prose of extraordinary if only incidental merit.

With Simeon Solomon, and not simply because drink and perversity ruined him, making him for the last thirty years of his life an outcast from even the least censorious circles of Bohemia, the decadence has begun in painting as in a poetical prose. The facts of his career are hardly familiar, his achievement, such as it was, has scarcely been considered with any seriousness since Swinburne's essay. The youngest son of a manufacturer of Leghorn hats who was the first Jew to be admitted a freeman of the City of London, Simeon was born at 3 Sandys Street, Bishopsgate Without, on the 9th of October, 1840. His sister Rebecca, herself an artist, and almost as much at the mercy of disastrous impulses, instructed him, with important artistic consequences, in Hebrew history and ritual. His elder brother Abraham, who had exhibited at the Royal Academy from his seventeenth year, who had developed suddenly in 1854 an originality of which earlier work gave no promise, and who, after a popular success in 1857 with 'Waiting for the Verdict,' had markedly gone off, taught Simeon drawing in his studio. As precocious as Abraham, and with a much subtler temperament, Simeon was in the Royal Academy schools at fifteen and in his eighteenth year showed at the Royal Academy his 'Isaac Offered.' There quickly followed 'the finely drawn and composed' 'Finding of Moses' of Thackeray's praise, a picture the novelist credited with 'a great intention,' 'The Child Jeremiah' and other paintings, with ten drawings illustrative of Jewish ceremonies, eight designs for 'The Song of Solomon' and eight for 'The Book of Ruth,' as well as illustrations in *Once a Week*. The influence of D. G. Rossetti, Burne-

ANGELI LAUDANTES

Morris Tapestry from Design by Burne-Jones

Jones and Swinburne, with perhaps some anxiety to get clear of the purely Hebraic, then turned him towards classical subjects. The admirable 'Bacchus' of 1867 aroused the ardent admiration of Walter Pater, and the earlier and slightly later work, together with his very remarkable prose composition, 'A Vision of Love revealed in Sleep,' were eulogized by Swinburne in the *Dark Blue* in 1871. But, after showing 'The Toilet of a Roman Lady,' 1869, 'Love Bound and Wounded,' 1870, 'Judith and her Attendant,' 1872, Simeon Solomon collapsed into ways of life in which he produced little but those drawings, sanguines many of them, which he did in an hour or two for a few shillings, and which are still common in the windows of the baser dealers. At one time he was an exceptionally ill-recompensed pavement artist in Bayswater. Latterly, he was almost always lodged in St Giles's workhouse, and it was there that, three months after having been found unconscious in Great Turnstile, he died of heart failure on the 14th of August, 1905.

Limited as he was, extremely monotonous as he became in the last twenty years of his life, weak as was his drawing, Simeon Solomon was a man of rare genius. Nor was his range quite so narrow as examination of his hack work suggests. I have seen a drawing of his, done a few years before his collapse, a hasty enough sketch in chalk of the head of a child, in which, out of an almost uncontoured face, there look those eyes, without a thought behind them yet arousing thought in us, that are the authentic eyes of a child. With those eyes and an irresolute, half-petulant mouth, it is a thing in one way meaningless, in another with the whole meaning of childhood. But, of course, as a rule Simeon Solomon has only too much meaning in his refined, tenuous commerce with symbols that may seem at one moment those of sanctity and at another those of lust. Between these extremes, there are those pictures and drawings in which, from time to time, Solomon has reproduced without comment the stolid, sombre faces of rabbis or Greek priests intent on their ritual, and others in which ritual is rendered with a decadent appreciation and in which he becomes almost an illustrator for some of the Roman Catholic poems of Ernest Dowson and Lionel Johnson. But, in a final choice of what was most significant in this artist, we may well select those designs in which weary, lovely faces yearn to each other with epicene passion in some moment of wakening or relapse into sleep, and if one picture is to suffice, it might be that reproduced as frontispiece to this volume.

Burne-Jones, in his modesty, in the earnestness which underlies and overlies the fun so carefully kept out of his work, is an artist who proposed by taking thought to add a cubit to his stature. Aware, when he had emerged from discipleship to Rossetti, of his inadequacy as a draughtsman, he proceeded, at the urging, I seem to have somewhere heard or read, of Watts, but in obedience really to his own conscience, to develop a very careful, delicate, and elaborate method of drawing. He appears never to have doubted that his progress here was all gain, never to have suspected the truth that in art no man is the better for an irrelevant merit however honourably acquired. His work, fundamentally, had no need of that draughtsmanship, which remains a conscious and somewhat timid accomplishment, never becoming a natural and indispensable means of expression, used with the easy vigour of a master who puts his hand on a familiar instrument. The picture, beautifully conceived in other terms, has all that draughtsmanship applied to it, with a piety one must respect, with a certain incidental success, but after all without necessity. At best, the draughtsmanship gives one a separable pleasure; often it is a sheer irrelevancy. And all that loving care to make each square inch of canvas charming in colour and surface, excellent as is its motive and pleasing as is usually the result, betrays a misunderstanding, we need not say of art, but at least of his own genius. For Burne-Jones was not of those, not all of them great masters, with whom line and colour and surface can be adequately eloquent. He had an angel as some have had a devil; an angel, somewhat ineffectual as the robust may think, without any urgent or indeed very specific message; and his true success was but to make us aware of that gracious presence, a presence, not a power, at pause, and so pure as to be almost devoid of character.

XII

THE closeness and the duration of Swinburne's association with Rossetti's group have constantly been exaggerated. After a minute study of his career, some of the results of which I have summarized in another book, I am convinced that Pre-Raphaelitism was an interruption in Swinburne's natural literary development. Nearly all the main artistic enthusiasms of Swinburne can be dated back to his twelfth, his thirteenth or his fourteenth year. At the moment when, in 1857 and at Oxford, he was brought into contact with Rossetti, William Morris and Burne-Jones, he was deeply engaged in imitative work preparatory to the achievements of his brilliant prime, and his models were not those peculiarly honoured in Rossetti's circle. At that moment, and later, he was composing, with an unparalleled mimetic art and almost incredible self-denial, dramas in which the defects no less than the merits of Fletcher were exactly reproduced, without the slightest infusion of modern or distinctively Swinburnian lyricism. In 1857-9 he was meditating or writing such pieces as ' The Laws of Corinth,' ' Laugh and Lie Down,' ' The Loyal Servant,' dramas on a model with which no one in the Rossetti circle was familiar. He was absorbed also in the study of Border ballads, with a juster enthusiasm for the starkness of the original poetry, so far as it could be divined through the corruptions and improvements to which it had been subjected, than Rossetti ever felt. He was devoted to Landor, to Hugo, writers alien to his new friends, and had already entered on his passionately sympathetic study of Æschylus.

Encountering the members of the Rossetti circle, he was

temporarily drawn aside from his true course, by Morris rather than Rossetti, in 1857-8, and until 1860-1 was periodically doing work under their influence.

The least pictorial and particularizing of our poets, Swinburne had no real sympathy with Pre-Raphaelitism, strictly so-called; but he had an ardent admiration for what by 1857 was developing out of it. To be sure, as I have already said, it was a thing rather beside his own purpose, and though his admiration for his new friends was maintained, with but the slightest modification, to the end of his life, Rossettian and Morrisian influences can hardly be detected in his work after 1864 or 1865, and an even earlier terminal date might be hazarded.

Stepping a little aside from his own course, he placed himself for the first two or three of those six or seven years at the feet rather of the bluff and accessible William Morris than at those of the then aloof Rossetti. His very earliest extant poem, 'A Vigil,' out of which, when a certain Baudelairean element had been added, grew 'The Leper' of the first series of *Poems and Ballads*, was Morris with only a faint difference. Here are the unpublished verses of the first draft, almost all of them deleted when the piece was refashioned:

> The night grows very old: almost
> One hears the morning's feet move on.
> That flower is like a lily's ghost
> On the black water—only one.
>
> I thought she was not dying; feel
> How cold her naked feet are grown!
> I dare not either sit or kneel;
> The flesh is stiffened to the bone.
>
> I kissed these feet; never again
> Will she kiss me or any man.

Now she seems quiet though the pain
Has left her very forehead wan.

I fear that she will turn or speak
To me, as yesterday she did;
Those are not tear-stains on her cheek,
Nor wrinkles on her eye's white lid.

She said ' Be kind to me, I grow
So tired without you, I shall die
If you say nothing '; even so,
And she is dead now verily.

I wonder if she could just move
That shut close mouth and speak at all,
If she would say ' I did not love.'
How heavily her gown's folds fall!

Nay I will shut across her breast
Those thin grey palms held out so straight;
It hurts not me to let her rest
A little; also I can wait.

I am grown blind with all these things.
It may be now she hath in sight
A better knowledge; still there clings
The old question, Will not God do right?

The influence of Morris appears, sometimes more decisively, in many other early pieces held back by Swinburne from print, in ' The Death of Rudel ' and ' Rudel in Paradise,' in the fragment, apparently written in 1859,[1] beginning:

[1] This piece exists on the back of the MS. of one of the quasi-Elizabethan sonnets which Mr Wise and Sir Edmund Gosse printed for private circulation as *Undergraduate Sonnets* in 1918, but was not there reproduced in print. One of these sonnets, utterly unlike its fellows, is purely Rossettian, and fixes 1859 as the date when Rossetti became more influential with Swinburne than Morris.

𝔘𝔫𝔡𝔢𝔯𝔤𝔯𝔞𝔡𝔲𝔞𝔱𝔢 𝔓𝔞𝔭𝔢𝔯𝔰,

1858.

"And gladly wolde we learn and gladly teach."

CHAUCER.

OXFORD:

PRINTED AND PUBLISHED BY W. MANSELL, HIGH STREET.

F

As she sits in her father's house,
Full many thoughts there lie asleep
Under the patience of her brows,
Under her eyes so dear and deep.

Again, the other and more intense Morris, the author of ' Sir Peter Harpdon's End,' is found affecting Swinburne in ' The Queen's Tragedy,' which was written in 1859-60, and remained in manuscript till in 1919 Mr Wise caused thirty copies to be printed for private use. It should be added, however, that both in phrasing and in versification this piece shows less dependence on Morris than the poems just mentioned.

But the composition to which we must mainly direct ourselves is the first printed of Swinburne's poems, ' Queen Yseult,' Canto I of which appeared in *Undergraduate Papers*.

To what was most distinctive in that development out of a short-lived Pre-Raphaelitism, that phase of Romanticism associated with the names of Rossetti, Christina Rossetti, William Morris, Burne-Jones, no substantial contribution was made by Swinburne. But moving for a while after them, then for a while parallel to them, rather than exactly with them, he supplemented their efforts in several important respects. For one thing, he and he alone in some sort linked Victorian English with the slightly earlier French Romanticism. He was till 1862, when Hugo's thanks for his championship deprived him of all feeling for the master's limitations, the disciple of the chief French Romantic, and for the next forty years that master's idolatrous worshipper. He was the earliest English admirer of Baudelaire, of Gautier. Rossetti and Morris may have remained unaware of the importance of this flank movement by Swinburne, and indeed its importance was not clear till some twenty-five or thirty years later, but it did a good deal, in time, to diminish the isolation of the Victorian Romantics, to encourage a view of them according to which they, simply as Romantics had great though remote and imperfectly recognized allies in European literature. With the acclimatization of exotics, they began to look less alien.

Then Swinburne provided that which English Romanticism had lacked since the death of Shelley, an extravagant lyrical passion for liberty, a vehement sympathy with liberty-seeking movements throughout the world. Rossetti, moved once to the noble sonnet on the refusal of aid between nations, was profoundly incurious about politics. Morris, ceasing eventually to be the idle singer of an empty day, became a very active and rather pathetic Socialist, wasting his time on the dreariest people, but had no Shelleyan impulse, only, at bottom, a craftsman's discontent with conditions unfavourable to good craftsmanship. Through Swinburne, so far as he could be taken for a typical member of the group, it was linked not only vaguely to French Romanticism, but to the great age of English Romanticism.

The claims thus made for Swinburne should, however, be qualified at two points. Impressive as was the success in 1865 of *Atalanta in Calydon*, it had been preceded by Christina Rossetti's victory with *Goblin Market*. Again, it cannot be doubted that the scandal of the *Poems and Ballads* in 1866 was prejudicial to the group, and it is improbable that Rossetti would have suffered in 1871 if ' Laus Veneris ' and ' Anactoria ' and ' Dolores ' had not resulted in the formation of a kind of vigilance organization.

On the other hand, it must be urged that, at any rate from 1867, when Swinburne began to contribute critical prose to the *Fortnightly Review*, he did more than anyone else to prepare the fittest part of the public for appreciation of the work of the group. Had he not brought his association with the *Spectator*, where he had defended Meredith's *Modern Love* and Baudelaire's poems, to an end by a double hoax, or had Moxon's project of a periodical to be edited by Swinburne not been abandoned, the general body of readers might well have been brought before 1870 into a frame of mind reasonably sympathetic. For the early criticism of Swinburne, as we have it in the papers on Hugo, Meredith, Baudelaire, Théophile, and the *Fortnightly* essays on Arnold and Morris, was not only more lucid than much of the work of his later life; it expressed a highly contagious enthusiasm, and secured an emotional response even where its argument was not likely to be altogether effective.

XIII

JAMES THOMSON was of no group, was in truth among the most solitary of our poets, but he may be seen now and then on the fringes of the circle, consulting with William Michael Rossetti about the animal stretched at the feet of the Melancholia, with the result that he alters

> With the poor creature for dissection brought

into

> With the keen wolf-hound sleeping undistraught.

It is characteristic of him that, understanding the Melancholia better than Dürer himself, he does not know whether it is a sheep awaiting dissection or a wolf-hound that lies at her feet. He is constantly the victim of 'education,' without the peasant's security or the scholar's. He has, intermittently, a great style of his own, surpassing Dante Gabriel Rossetti himself in the filling of lines with sonorous Latinate polysyllabic phrases; he can set the walls of his chapel of disbelief rocking with the reverberation of his tremendous double rhymes; he can accumulate the symbols of disaster with extraordinary resource so that when it seems impossible to add anything which shall not diminish the total effect there shall indeed be some dreadful gain,

> As if blacker night could dawn on night
> With tenfold gloom on moonless night unstarred.

But his only security is in monotony. The moment he escapes from

70

The City of Dreadful Night to walk otherwise than in a circle, or under changeful skies, his style becomes uncertain, a mixture of Shelley, Heine, Browning and refined vulgarism.

If he could have either acquired or escaped education! For Thomson, in that trying, too-much-neglected part of his work which celebrates Cockney gaieties, was attempting things very well worth doing, of a real novelty. He really had divined that the choice is not simply between the poetry of great passions and what James Hogg, with an excellent contempt, called ' college poetry,' but that there remains the poetry of light impulses and caprices and casual adventures, and that poetry may come and go in an idle mind like a tune and the muse be as the girl a young man picks up and loves for Rochester's ' livelong minute.' For what he was trying to do in ' Sunday up the River' Thomson had every qualification except ignorance or culture. Again and again he is within an inch of positive success in that difficult enterprise, but some damnable half-knowledge of what is correct gets in the way, the laughter turns to giggling, the sentiment to sentimentality. Not that there are no achievements. Several of his slighter pieces have real Cockney happiness; at least two sing exquisitely; but the poem that should blend perfectly all that realism and light romance remains unwritten.

For all that, when we have done praising the sombre and majestic *City of Dreadful Night* and the sometimes almost Keatsian Arabic story, we should salute Thomson for his part in an attempt, begun even more uncertainly by Leigh Hunt, continued in other ways by Browning, culminating, perhaps, in the learned and perverse invalid's amusement of Jules Laforgue, to make poetry modern. This, too, is a part of Romanticism, the discovery of the romance of everyday, though it may need a certain disillusionment with romance for complete success in it.

XIV

In considering the work of a group of artists who have been thought of, and excusably, as given over to a languid luxury and to the too deliberate accumulation of precious accessories, it is well to emphasize, for their corrective value, those exceptional achievements in which hand and soul have co-operated in the service of an austerer ideal. And since it is eminently Rossetti who is liable to misunderstanding, I will take his case. For the destruction of all the half-truths about his painting I need only cite two of his successes, ' Arthur's Tomb ' and ' The Beloved.'

The small early water-colour shows us Rossetti at once at the height of his energy and in fullest possession of the power of solving an emotional problem strictly in the terms of the painter. There is no question here of ' the crisis of a face.' The tragedy of the situation of Lancelot and Guinevere, meeting by the wronged king's tomb, is not merely conveyed to us by its reflection in mournful eyes, by the suggestion of the words that would come from lips that have tasted forbidden fruit and learned to loathe its sweetness. Here is no single figure within a symbolical setting. The thing is truly a composition. That it is so small is a triumphant proof of Rossetti's genius. Into those few inches, with an art for once not inferior to that which went to the making of the ' moment's monument ' of a sonnet, and with far more vehemence than we find in any of the sonnets, Rossetti has forced the crouching and menacing figure of Lancelot, the uncloistered, drawn and recoiling figure of Guinevere, the horizontal sculptured figure of Arthur, making the tacit commentary which the dead make on the acts of the living; and then, with a magnificent stroke of designer's genius, he has crushed them down with the stiff, incumbent, stark bough of the tree. The picture is, as it was resolutely intended to be, without relief. The eye yearns for the consolation of the perpendicular, and in vain. Here, indeed, are those who are between the upper and the nether mill-stones; here are, in truth, heads upon which the ends of the world are come.

It is a tortured picture: the one picture of Rossetti's comparable for intensity and ruthless compression with the poem by William Morris, itself unique in the poet's work. But my concern with it here is to bring home to the reader the completeness of Rossetti's success in conveying the emotional tension through tension of design where, going his more usual way, he might but have suggested it through facial expression.

And now look at that other picture, one of the few of its period for which the beautiful and abominable Fanny Schott was not his model. For the most part 'The Beloved' is simply the typical Rossetti picture, only done better than usual. But the left-centre of the lower part of the canvas is filled with the likeness of a negro child holding a vase of roses, and there, in that head, with its consummate modelling, Rossetti for once is with the greatest masters. It is true that the realism of that head makes war on the almost uncontoured, vaguely poetic face of the bride herself, and that for all its wealth of colour and such incidental felicities as the success in making us almost hear the singing of the two principal bridesmaids, the whole is not quite satisfying. But if anyone thinks that Rossetti could not paint the human animal with understanding alike of osseous structure and of the pathos of the soul unconscious of its cage, let him look at that negro child and learn the enormity of his error.

Like every Puritan who is also an artist, Holman Hunt is constantly being driven to compromises. He puzzled the Jew dealer who commissioned ' The Scapegoat ': ' I wanted a nice religious bicture, and he has bainted me a great goat.' But his intellectual position is not a puzzle only because indefensible compromises between the desire of the eyes, the prime motive of painting, and an essentially unimaginative resolve to serve God directly, by denying the half of what He has created, have been so common among us. Blake can say with perfect composure that the nakedness of woman and the pride of the peacock and the lust of the goat are parts of the glory of God; it has to be a scapegoat before it is to Hunt's purpose. His ' Scapegoat ' is a miracle. As Ford Madox Brown said of it at the time when it was first shown, ' it requires to be seen to be believed in.' ' Only then can it be believed how, by the might of genius, out of an old goat and some saline incrustations, can be made one of the most tragic and impressive works in the annals of art.' At the other extreme of Holman Hunt's achievement is the thing on which he worked for half·a century, ' The Lady of Shalott.' The picture is not so great as the original design for it. It is not great at all; for it is the result neither of a grappling with earthly reality nor of imaginative vision of unearthly reality, but the intricate and opulent record of fancy, working on the level of Tennyson's fancy. The Puritan, unable to take romance perfectly earnestly, and constitutionally incapable of frivolity, has ended in this solemn game with the accessories of romance, the Rapunzel hair, the enchanted mirror, and the rest. But it has its charm, or rather its separable charms, and is not, despite the control of the beautiful original design, so much a picture as a gallery in which we may see every excellence, except the tragic, to which Holman Hunt could attain.

Since Holman Hunt in a candid and valuable book explained the immediate origin of Pre-Raphaelitism, there is a danger that he may be taken for an authority on its remoter origin. The break with the past of English painting was not quite so sharp as he thought. In his book, which does not lack pungency, he sums up the equability of Mulready as ' the equality of empty scales.' The jibe is not

Cleopatra

FREDERICK SANDYS

without excuse. But can anyone tell me what essential difference there is between the average early Pre-Raphaelite picture and such a picture by Mulready as ' The Sonnet '?

I will quote Swinburne in honour of Frederick Sandys, who alone among the English painters and draughtsmen of his time had full command of tragedy:

Among the drawings [in the Academy of 1868] are two studies by Mr Sandys, both worthy of the high place held by the artist. One is a portrait full of force and distinction, drawn as perhaps no other man among us can draw; the other, a woman's face, is one of his most solid and splendid designs; a woman of rich, ripe, angry beauty, she draws one warm long lock of curling hair through her full and moulded lips, biting it with bared bright teeth, which add something of a tiger's charm to the sleepy and couching passion of her fair face. . . . Mr Sandys' picture of ' Medea ' is well enough known by this time, wherever there is any serious knowledge of art, to claim here some word of comment, not less seasonable than if it were now put forward to grace the great show of the year. Like Coriolanus, the painter might say if he would that it is his to banish the judges, his to reject the ' common cry ' of academics. For this, beyond all doubt, is as yet his masterpiece. Pale as from poison, with the blood drawn back from her very lips, agonized in face and limbs with the labour and the fierce contention of old love with new, of a daughter's love with a bride's, the fatal figure of Medea pauses a little on the funereal verge of the wood of death, in act to pour a blood-like liquid into the soft opal-coloured hollow of a shell. The future is hard upon her, as a cup of bitter poison set close to her mouth; the furies of Absyrtus, the furies of her children, rise up against her from the unrisen years; her eyes are hungry and helpless, full of a fierce and raging sorrow. Hard by her, henbane and aconite and nightshade thrive and grow full of fruit and death; before her fair feet the bright-eyed toads engender after their kind. Upon the golden ground behind is wrought in allegoric decoration the likeness of the ship Argo, with other emblems of the tragic things of her life. The picture is grand alike for wealth of symbol and solemnity of beauty.

It was for a drawing by Sandys that Swinburne, almost impromptu, produced that minor masterpiece of decadent poetry, 'Cleopatra.' George Meredith, then, as again at the close of life, cordial in admiration, but constitutionally disqualified for appreciation of work in that temper, persuaded him that it was no more than a farrago of the commonplaces of his poetical style, and Swinburne never reprinted it. Too relaxed in mood and too curiously wrought in structure to rank with his very best work, hardly appropriate to the fundamentally dignified drawing, 'Cleopatra' is all the same a thing of beauty and of a certain importance in the evolution of decadent art. Beyond question it is the model for Oscar Wilde's poem, 'The Sphinx,' and it gave some hint to Walter Pater for the most famous, not the most characteristic, passage of his prose, and it prepared an atmosphere for the men of the 'nineties.

XV

THAT the Pre-Raphaelites and certain other admirable artists of the period were rejected or very grudgingly acknowledged by the Royal Academy is a story told and retold to weariness: the point that has been missed is that the Academicians, eager for an art of illustration, flouted the greatest illustrators of that age, the greatest group of illustrators England has had in any one decade.

The wealth of noble or charming work done during the 'sixties, mostly for quite popular periodicals or for books addressed to the general public, is astonishing. Look at the *Cornhill*, at *Once a Week*, at the *Sunday Magazine*, at *Good Words*, and at such books as Willmott's *Sacred Poetry*, 1862, and the Dalziel *Arabian Nights!* The engravers, with the exception of W. J. Linton, a charming small poet, an exceptional translator from the French, as well as a master of engraving, are given to worsening or weakening the line, and sometimes falsify the expression altogether. The Dalziel brothers, one of them a good artist, all of them quick to discern artistic merit, are very far from being irreproachable.

> O woodman spare that block,
> O gash not anyhow!
> It took ten days by clock,
> I'd fain protect it now.
> *Chorus*—Wild laughter from Dalziel's Workshop.

Thus Rossetti, who, however, set the engravers a sometimes almost impossible task by employing ink, pencil, brush on the one intricate drawing. On the whole, and despite an audacious personal method,

77

invented in desperation with his first drawing on the wood, it was Frederick Sandys who suffered most.

Millais was the king of these illustrators; and it is the Millais escaped from the original P.R.B., not yet degenerate; it is he—not Menzel or any member of the P.R.B.—who is inspiration and exemplar to most of the illustrators of the period, to most of those who matter. Those designs of his in the *Parables of Our Lord*, 1863,[1] the consummate Prodigal Son, the grim and never-to-be-forgotten Tares, the beautifully composed Sower, with its defined rocky foreground, are models of which no man with eyes and ambition could be heedless. There is, even out of the wonderful decade, not much that can reasonably be set on a level with the work of Millais as an illustrator. How others would choose I do not know, but for my part if called upon to match the greatest of the Millais Parable drawings on their own ground, I should without hesitation pick Ford Madox Brown's magnificent ' Elijah and the Widow's Son ' out of the much later published *Bible Gallery* of the Dalziels. With perfect plausibility, the illustration is designed step-wise, descending from the top right-hand corner; above and to the extreme right there is the figure of the prophet, charged with character as no other man in that generation could have charged him, and immediately below, held forth by the prophet, is the boy, and then, at precisely the interval desired by the eye, there is the kneeling figure of the widow. The interest is concentrated where it should be, but balance is secured by the treatment.

Probably, however, if there is to be anyone set up against Millais the illustrator by virtue of his work as a whole that man must be A. Boyd Houghton. Certain of his paintings, particularly one of a group of Volunteers in the early days of that movement, have points of likeness to some of the paintings of Ford Madox Brown; have, at any rate, some of the same honesty, the same willingness to accept

[1] Commonly dated 1864, but actually issued in 1863.

St Agnes' Eve

MILLAIS

a comic element in the material. In the drawings done by Boyd Houghton for the periodicals of the 'sixties, for the Dalziels' *Arabian Nights*, 1863-5, and for *Don Quixote*, what was impatient and sardonic in the man becomes evident enough. Swift and summarizing, he gets on to his block with an unusual economy the results of an observation that has captured the characteristic thing and passed by everything else. Nearly all the drawings of Oriental subjects show an unparaded observation of things commonly missed. Boyd Houghton knows, for instance, that people who have gone barefooted all their days walk otherwise than those who have taken off their shoes in the studio, and there is a drawing of his, an Eastern ploughman seen from behind at the moment of checking his cattle, in which there is almost as much science in the drawing of the small of the back and the buttocks as Degas put into a ballet-girl straining at the bar. Outside the books, he seldom did anything better than two early drawings in the *Sunday Magazine*, ' John Baptist ' and ' The Parable of the Sower '; for the best of his more elaborate work one must look at the design in the British Museum of ' Reading the Chronicles,' which has his customary energy and sense of character, with a special skill in the grouping of the figures about the regal, reclining listener and the crouched, expository reader.

For all the great qualities of the Millais and Madox Brown and Boyd Houghton drawings, I for one would rather possess a complete set of the Frederick Sandys than a complete set of any other of these masters of illustration. Sandys was limited, in range and in the quantity of his production: a great reputation rests on less than thirty designs, in which three or four emotional motifs are repeated. All those designs were done in less than fifteen years, and then, the heat he caught from Rossetti dying out of him, he became cold. What there is to show for the last decades of a long life no one need trouble to enquire, though dignity and a precise draughtsmanship, his birthright and his acquisition, he preserved to the end. But in several of his drawings, as in all his major paintings, there is a grandeur more natural than that of any contemporary. It is Watts who is the typical grand artist of the Victorian period; and, with his consciousness of being the heir of all the artistic ages, his choice of noble or at any rate distinguished subjects, his grave approach, he has nobility, sometimes only of intention, often purchased at a cost to sheer painting and draughtsmanship. Capable, as he proved often enough, of painting the sitter as he is and yet educing greatness, he will evade the challenge to a certainly not inadequate technique in a lofty refusal of what he has come to think a trivial particularity; and, as regards a woman's dress, determined that it shall not date, will generalize it into a meaningless cloak of nudity. But Frederick Sandys, so much smaller and more limited an artist, in his brief best period had a native nobility, not of intention but of spirit, that comes through to us in almost every one of his designs. It is perfectly naturally that he turns to Greek tragic legend and Norse sagas for subjects; the heroic is his element.

The engravers damaged almost every one of the thirteen drawings he did for *Once a Week*. The very beautiful ' Amor Mundi,' done in 1865 as an illustration for Christina Rossetti's poem in Cassell's *Shilling Magazine*, was yet more beautiful in the original. He himself said that the ' Danaë,' in the *Hobby-Horse* in 1888, was the first satisfactory engraving he had had; it is a good engraving, but see what has been done to the shadow on the upper lip! ' Proud Maisie,' too great a thing for the poem, though that is the one authentic poem written by Sir Walter Scott, survived each of the several treatments it received; of that and the ' Morgan le Fay,' in the *British Architect*, 1879, it may safely be said that we have them as they should be for the simple reason that even Sandys could not have conceived them more greatly, executed them more nobly.

Sandys, who did more than one drawing for Swinburne during the few years of their friendship, should have been employed to illustrate *Atalanta in Calydon* and then the northern narrative poetry of William Morris. Dante Gabriel Rossetti was the natural illustrator of his own poetry and of some of Christina's, and one of his drawings for her ' You Should Have Wept Her Yesterday,' in *The Prince's Progress*, 1866, is a most subtly beautiful and faithful translation into design of her verse. But for the slighter and blither part of her poetry, for those minute and delightful poems in which she is richer even than Herrick, there was but one man, Arthur Hughes, who collaborated with her so happily in ' Speaking Likenesses.' In his drawings for William Allingham, whose verse was so fortunate with Rossetti and Hughes as illustrators; in such drawings for periodicals as ' Sun Comes, Moon Comes,' done for *Good Words*, in 1871; in the delicious painting of ' April Love,' full of tender hesitation, full of the spirit of girlhood, a beautiful nature is seen expressing itself. In the *Tom Brown* illustrations, done for a namesake who was no relation, there is inevitably a descent into the robust commonplaces of the subject. The truth about Hughes is that he was in his own modest way one of ' Love's lovers.' Others in that generation, Rossetti especially, brought Love the gifts of the Magi, were celebrants of the mysteries of sacred and profane passion; Hughes came at dawn or twilight with the simplest offerings and to an innocent, unritualled worship. At a time when they made books like Willmott's *Sacred Poetry*, a horrid book if it were not for some of the contents and such drawings as those by Sandys, they should have made, with more simplicity, an anthology of love lyrics for Hughes to illustrate. Actually, he had the illustrating of *Enoch Arden*, of which we may say what Luttrell said of the *Italy* of Rogers, that ' it would have been dished but for the plates.'

XVI

As regards poetry, the new men who mattered were followers of
Rossetti and his closest associates: as regards painting, the best of
the secondary, mostly younger, men were influenced by the
earlier, the more strictly Pre-Raphaelite work, rather than by the
mature Rossetti and by Burne-Jones. It must be possible, since it
has been done, to write about Strudwick and Byam Shaw, but not
for me; I can but apologize for my incapacity, and throw back to
those others, several of them strongly affected by Millais. And here
it becomes necessary to say more of Millais himself. What he
was for a little while, in contact with Hunt and Rossetti and Madox
Brown, is matter for a proud page in the history of English painting
and illustration. Almost the last of the old Millais, with much of the
best of what the new was to be, is in the sketches he made during
his Scottish tour with the Ruskins, an episode ending with the
transformation of Mrs Ruskin into Mrs Millais. The marriage was
announced in the *Leader*, July 7th, 1855, under the heading
' Deaths ': not on account of the marriage, it was virtually the death
of the great artist, the birth of the salmon-fishing, hearty Philistine.

That poetry went out of Millais is a commonplace, but seldom
has it been indicated quite how. The affair, it seems to me, was not
simply one of pot-boiling. The radical trouble with the new Millais
was that he began to provide prosaic, circumstantial justification for
the presence and the occupations of the people in his pictures. Now
with great painters the figure, the poise and gesture, the accessories,
the background, need no rational explanation of their coming together within the frame. Monna Lisa in that strange landscape, the

Melancholia amidst that ' strange alliance ' of properties, or that tailor at his workaday task, all offer us, for immediate acceptance and complete satisfaction, an inexplicable inner harmony between the figure and its setting. Millais himself has done it, in ' Autumn Leaves,' where there is no thought of telling us why the figures are occupied as they are, only a profound lyrical impulse to render the mystery of a simple, infinitely significant action in the setting it makes for itself. But that other Millais! The fireman is on the seventeenth rung of the ladder, or the doctor by the bedside, or the nuns are posed with practicable shovels by the grave, *because*, you see . . . They can account for their presence and their precise doings, at the moment at which he has accosted them, as glibly and in as matter-of-fact a way as the accused at the police-court, and might be put in the background in plan, with exhibits A and B and C. Millais has forgotten that the body of man possessing the body of woman, a mother's arm going round her child, a sower's gesture as he scatters seed, are more than movements to satisfy a particular moment's lust, to mitigate a child's momentary fear, to ensure a crop in the five-acre field; that they are things eternally significant, parts of a rhythm that began before the individual life and will persist after it, and that it is an abominable triviality to relate the movement only to its immediate excuse.

XVII

SOMETHING of the earlier and incomparably nobler Millais, or of Holman Hunt, or of Ford Madox Brown is to be discerned in the work of most of those whom I now take without much concern for the order of their appearance. The precision of John Brett, as he goes about the difficult business of extending the early Pre-Raphaelite method to landscape, may not mean very much to us. 'The Stone Breaker' has some unpleasant chalkiness of colour in parts, though the cliffs in the background compensate for that, and would for almost anything. The more frequently cited landscape by him seems in my memory of it a thing done from without, in a serious but unimpassioned challenge to a skill that is three parts patience. But look at the 'Lady with a Dove,' in the Tate! It is in all respects a small thing, and I do not know that one would care to see a dozen things of the sort in any one gallery. But the minute finish has, for once, a purely artistic justification, not merely the mostly irrelevant and moral excuse offered by Holman Hunt; finish of that sort, if you will consider the little picture carefully, was dictated by the scale of the thing, by the firm and daintily chiselled profile of the Lady, by the perching dove; and with how grave a happiness, almost as of a masterpiece by Whistler, though without any suggestion of his way with the brush, have the grey and the beautiful black of the dress come together!

Two other workers in detail at once justify themselves. Martineau's 'The Last Day in the Old Home' extorts from detail, without effort, all that it can yield of the emotion proper to his subject, and the apparent prose domesticity of the picture should not blind any-

one to the imagination in the chief figure to the right, the excellently
observed spendthrift, elegant, anxious, discovering, as his kind will,
a hope for the better day as he raises his glass, or to the unobtrusive
pathos of his little son imitating the father. A faint suggestion of
wax-work diminishes the pleasure given by the ' Chatterton ' of
Henry Wallis, with its logical, rather too logical, accumulation of
accessories, without enough hint of the indifferent movement of a life
that will go on though poet-forgers kill themselves in garrets. The
hair, where the light falls on it, and the wrinkled rug beneath the
corpse, are the work of a hand that had felt textures.

Others perhaps not more remote from the earlier Pre-Raphaelite
ideals might be brought into the discussion, but I pass to some more
obviously related to the group of the 'fifties. W. S. Burton's
' Wounded Cavalier,' for work done at twenty-six, has an assurance
in dealing with detail truly remarkable; and Charles Alston Collins,
Wilkie's brother, in ' Convent Thoughts,' announced an artist who,
with persistence and the likely enough discovery that the human
body is flexible, would have mattered. The ' Burd Helen ' of W. L.
Windus, showed, among other merits, a rare feeling for the type of
face requisite for the conveyance of his matter, the heartless lover
being an inspired, surprising, at once convincing, piece of casting
for a part which with most other painters would have been filled so
very differently. But it is ' Too Late,' with the consummately rendered face of the consumption-stricken girl and the admirable gawk
of a younger sister gazing up, in an incomplete comprehension of
tragedy, at the man who covers his face, that is his masterpiece.
Seen in a catalogue, the title would be a warning; but there was
never a picture of the sort that less needed a title.

Whether anyone has reckoned in George Wilson in numbering
the host of those who took some tinge from the Pre-Raphaelites, I
do not remember. If he belongs to them, it is only in spirit, and
perhaps not altogether in spirit even, for he went to Shelley where

they went to Keats. It is in his picture of a very Shelley-like poet making his bewildered way through the thorny labyrinth of life that he comes nearest to achievement. There is, however, a great gulf between such gracious, derivative symbolism and the energetic, original symbolism, at one glorious moment barely inferior to Blake's, which bodies forth the ideas of Nettleship. He took up eventually with alcohol and lions, getting, one must hope, some comfort out of each as a man, but getting out of neither as an artist the violence of the subject. A drunkard's picture by Henri de Toulouse-Lautrec, and Ward's not quite sane fight between a snake and a tiger, put that Nettleship in his unimportant place. The other, the author of the superb ' Jacob Wrestling with the Angel,' Jacob held in the hollow of the Angel's hand, is a master, doing a tremendous thing with an unfaltering energy; and there is reason to believe, with the dubiously reported eulogies of Rossetti and Browning ringing in our ears, that the lost design of ' God Creating Evil,' a woman and a tiger issuing from the Creator's forehead, was the sublimest thing done since Blake. There is something more to Nettleship's account, that strange ' Head of Minos.' ' I would do my contours in iron, if I could,' said Géricault, expressing the ideal of a certain kind of painting. Well, here is drawing in iron. I cannot praise it. I can only refer the reader to a passage written by Swinburne, long before and without the least thought of Nettleship, in eulogy of the great French tragedies of George Chapman: a passage in which he sees stamped on those tragedies a single, superhuman face, implacable and terrific.

XVIII

NETTLESHIP did drawings, all of a certain imaginative power but
mostly unpleasing in line, for *The Epic of Women*, O'Shaughnessy's
first volume of verse, which was published in the same year as
Rossetti's *Poems*. When, four years later, there appeared *Music and
Moonlight*, O'Shaughnessy's work was done. He had had but little
to express, and from the first he has made it plain both that he was
derivative and that there was in his genius, for he had genius, a
flaw such as might be expected in one who had Irish blood in him
and was the son of Bulwer-Lytton. Something of Moore, faintly
perceptible in even so good a poem as ' The Fountain of Tears,'
and something tricky, which has been referred to Poe but is
explicable in terms of Bulwer-Lytton, may be found in all his
weaker work. But he had his inspirations, from the grave
and from a nostalgia of some faintly remembered life before
birth.

> Des voluptés interieures
> Le sourire mystérieux!

He has that attraction for us which is exercised most commonly in
life by the reminiscent smile of a woman, usually a quite empty-
minded woman, who is recalling, not the subtle experiences with
which our sensual imagination credits her, but trivialities. He has
the advantage over her, inevitably, for in art there is no luck of
features, that he really is remembering an exquisite thing, really is
listening to a secret song.

> But all the while within I hear
> A song I do not sing for fear—
> How sweet, how different a thing!

A poet for anthologists, he was nearly or quite ruined by the too enthusiastic Palgrave, and others have given us with a unanimity that is wearisome the best part of ' We are the Music-Makers ' and ' The Fountain of Tears.' They ought to give us ' Bisclaveret,' which in its treatment of the werewolf theme adds energy to his customary merits, and ' There is an earthly glimmer in the tomb,' the last lines of which have a security of style rare indeed in this improvising poet.

> While Memory, in some soft low monotone,
> Is pouring like an oil into mine ear
> The tale of a most short and hollow bliss,
> That I once throbbed, indeed, to call my own,
> Holding it hardly between joy and fear,—
> And how that broke, and how it came to this.

Philip Bourke Marston, allied to O'Shaughnessy, even more dependent on Rossetti and Swinburne, even more monotonous, was too fortunate in one way, too unfortunate in every other, to approach the success certainly within reach of his talent. The descendant of Marston, the Elizabethan, the son of Westland Marston, having ' Festus ' Bailey as godfather and Mrs Craik as godmother, almost adopted by Swinburne from the age of fourteen, he had ' advantages ' perilous to a nature not disposed to go its own way. For the rest, with partial blindness from the age of three, and total blindness from twenty, and with an almost unparalleled series of bereavements in his short life, he was far too much driven in on himself. It is impossible to read his many sonnets without sympathy with the man and respect for the craftsman, but in following Rossetti he forgot Rossetti's demand for ' fundamental brainwork '; and

when, most successfully in ' The Old Churchyard of Bonchurch,'
he followed Swinburne he forgot that the slightest check in such a
metre will be a jolt. But he was himself in writing

> I put my flower of song into thy hand,
> And turn my eyes away,—
> It is a flower from a most desolate land,
> Barren of sun and day,
> Even this life of mine.
> As two who meet upon a foreign strand,
> 'Twas mine with thee to stray,—
> I put this flower of song into thy hand
> And turn my eyes away,
> And look where no lights shine . . .

XIX

RICHARD WATSON DIXON, the most unfortunate in respect of recognition of the original Morris group, went unillustrated for all that his earlier work contains many invitations to the illustrator. 'St Mary Magdalene' reads like a poem made for a design by Rossetti. In other pieces there is such matter as this:

> Row ranged on row they came; the light of love
> Burned softly in their eyes, row ranged on row
> Of men in heavenly panoply, a grove
> Of violet plumes and lifted swords; below
> And through, 'twixt arm and shoulder, and between
> Plumed helm and helm, wild eyes and golden hair
> And passionate lips; with throngings here and there.

With something of Keats's pictorial gift, he has at times the very note of Keats, as in the beautiful ode 'To Summer':

> Yet thou must fall, sweet nurse of budded boughs.

There are the other odes, 'The Fall of the Leaf,' 'The Spirit Wooed,' the 'Ode on Advancing Age,' poems of a grave passion unrecognized in their own period and far too little recognized even to-day. There are certain lyrics, especially 'The Feathers of the Willow' with its wealth of autumnal symbols. And there is 'Mano,' too complicated in plot, but full of beautiful things, and a triumph of virtuosity in the use of *terza rima*.

His friend, Mr Robert Bridges, writing of the romantic quality of strangeness common to Blake and William Morris, has asked us to note how with Blake the strangeness falls to a subordinate rank, in service to a wider imagination and a more spiritual purpose, and has declared Dixon to be in this regard with Blake rather than Morris. A single brief lyric of Dixon's gives us almost all of Blake-like imagination that there was in him.

> Silent fell the rain
> To the earthly ground;
> Then arose a sound
> To complain.

The epithet ' earthly ' there; the wintered bird ' in his bewildered bower '; the ' drifted ' ring of the fallen leaves: Dixon is full of these unobtrusive felicities in poems which, written after he had emerged from Pre-Raphaelitism, may seem rather bare and flat at a first glance. With him the romantic impulse has been disciplined, by scholarship, by spiritual authority. He was the author of a great and disgracefully neglected history of the Church of England; his is an Anglican poetry, a poetry of spiritual romance poised between the Puritanism of Holman Hunt and the pagan Catholicism accepted, for purposes of art, by Dante Gabriel Rossetti.

XX

THE painters of the period worked in an atmosphere charged with the influences, and I use the plural advisedly, of Ruskin; and Rossetti, over and above what each member of the Pre-Raphaelite group owed to the empassioned preacher of sound and false doctrine, was for certain years under a heavy direct obligation.

I do not see how any critic can give us the complete truth about Ruskin. There are few things to be said by wisdom or folly about art which Ruskin did not somewhere say; and with equal plausibility and wealth of documentation he may be presented as the possessor of an almost unrivalled insight into new principles of painting and as a brutally bigoted amateur. Holman Hunt, I take it, understood Ruskin not much more than did the average intelligent reader of the period, and certainly the doctrine of mere reproduction would have been so congenial to Hunt the theorist, a smaller man than the artist, that the wiser message of Ruskin would have had little chance with him. But Ruskin, it is amusing to reflect, could declare the independence of painting in terms as uncompromising as those used by Whistler.

The most notable pronouncement, I suppose, but the brevity of life precludes the searching of the whole of Ruskin, is that, in the *Stones of Venice*, in which he says:

We are to remember, in the first place, that the arrangement of colours and tones is an art analogous to the composition of music, and entirely independent of the representation of facts.

We are far enough from the original theory of Pre-Raphaelitism

92

The Lady of Shalott

HOLMAN HUNT

there! Far also from the teaching of Ruskin himself on many other pages. In reading him it is almost always necessary to allow for the occasion, the particular audience, the mood or malady of an often petulant and sometimes deranged writer. How far the Pre-Raphaelites made the requisite allowances is hard to discover. They had him not as we have him, but in course of agitated development. He had begun to write art criticism, or magniloquent discourses on the nature of things with somewhat hastily chosen pictures as pretexts, long before Pre-Raphaelitism began, and before he himself knew quite whither he was tending. Much of his work was too propagandist or too much to some special occasion to allow of clear exposure of his whole position. And, in the main, he was a stimulant rather than a guide. But, his writings apart, simply as a private counsellor, he was for a while of great benefit to Rossetti.

One knows not how much to credit to Ruskin's wisdom, how much to his luck: there is evidence enough that his understanding of Rossetti was at certain times seriously at fault, and the final attempt of the smaller man to brow-beat the greater was painfully comic. Yet, for a while, Ruskin did Rossetti the great service of keeping him to the small things painted out of the inner heat of imagination when clients were tempting Rossetti to do single female heads out of his dreamy sensuality.

In the end, there was misunderstanding, not all of it the misunderstanding of hostility. We can but smile unhappily when the infinitely amiable Burne-Jones is a witness for Ruskin, defendant, against Whistler. No doubt Whistler took his liberties with Nature, but before he began to paint; the brush once in his hand, for the rendering of the fastidiously selected aspect of her, he had scruples more delicate than any known to Ruskin. And it was absurdly that the author of the words I have quoted from Ruskin, 'an art analogous to the composition of music,' clashed with the painter who went to music for the titles of his harmonies and symphonies; absurdly that Burne-Jones supported the Ruskin of caprice against the Ruskin who was a sage, and against Whistler. There need never have been a quarrel; I am sure, after study of the unedited documents, that if chance had not frustrated Swinburne's earlier effort to get Ruskin to Whistler's studio, there never would have been one. But Ruskin could not, in any event, have been continuously sympathetic even where Rossetti was concerned. In all his generosity in other ways, he wished to have not God's Rossetti but Ruskin's.

He was right about Rossetti for a while, preferring the little watercolours in which imagination rules to the luxuriously fanciful works in which, sometimes, Rossetti seems less to be rendering a subject than providing patrons with a typical Rossetti, instantly recognizable as such. For that while, he knew Rossetti better than Rossetti knew himself, but he was the smaller man of the two. It may sound blasphemous to say so; yet in art, in a final judgment, the immense range, the feverish, high-motived enthusiasm, the inexhaustible eloquence of a Ruskin count for little. They made him, after Carlyle, the chief influence of his age. But all that matters ultimately in art is the thing done in the faultless co-operation of hand and soul, not preachment, with whatever gift of tongues, about the aims of doing or the conditions of achievement.

There were very few in that period who were capable of full achievement. Indeed, though there were greater writers than these it sometimes seems to me that only Rossetti and Pater and Coventry Patmore, in their finest work, had that power of perfect adequacy, the effect with Pater, however, being often of an exact mosaic rather than of a beautiful thing cast, by a single act, as a whole. But all Rossetti's associates contributed to the new ideal of artistic perfection, of a purified and self-sufficing beauty; all had that vision which was Coleridge's when he wrote:

> She, she herself, and only she,
> Shone through her body visibly.

Beauty herself, inutile, disengaged from all the moral and social conditions of her acceptance by Ruskin or by the apostate Tennyson of ' The Palace of Art,' has had no such service from a group since then. If it was not in Ruskin so to serve her, at least he made all England aware of the religion of beauty.

XXI

VICTORIAN Romanticism by, or soon after, 1870 is condemned to death, but with an ' indefinite reprieve ' which proved to be long. Rossetti has hardly come completely before the general body of readers as a poet, Swinburne has hardly reached his highest lyrical achievement in the ardent and purified *Songs Before Sunrise*, when the period of decline begins.

I say decline, rather than decadence, because the latter word has too many meanings, some of which cannot be read into the decline till the 'nineties. What we see at the close of the epoch covered by this volume, as regards poetry, is first a thinning of the substance. In Marston, and still more in O'Shaughnessy, poetry becomes tenuous not so much through spiritualization as through lack of blood. A certain amount of Pre-Raphaelite colour is retained; there is a good deal that is superficially Rossettian and Swinburnian; but there is very seldom any of that ' fundamental brainwork,' that ' mental cartooning ' on which Rossetti insisted, and there is none of the energy, none of the humane enthusiasm of Swinburne. We discern the symptoms of an often graceful enough decline, with the establishment of a diction slightly too poetic to be the vehicle of the finest poetry. We see a process of thinning and weakening, but hardly any perversion. When perversion does appear it is, as it nearly always will be, first of all in technique, questions of technique being, though few can see or care to admit as much, absolutely fundamental. Hopkins, isolated except for the sympathy of Richard Watson Dixon, and later of Mr Robert Bridges, sets out in heroic and hopeless, yet after all not unrewarded, search of something not unlike that which Stéphane Mallarmé sought. He destroys the natural order of words, wrenches syntax, flouts punctuation in an endeavour to secure a coincidence between emotional, logical and metrical emphasis which can be attained, if at all, only for a few lines at a time. It is inadequate to say that he will speak only the language of incantations; he wishes to get out of words not a spell which shall cause the rose to blossom or the bird to fly on his page, but, instantaneously, petals where the type has been imposed, the very swoop of wings in the lines. In equal isolation, with less skill and less hazardous ambition, James Thomson, in his slighter work, is trying to be modern, to be casual, the poet of whims and lucky encounters and undignified entertainments. Later there will be Henley, whose significance as a link between the faintly Pre-Raphaelite or ' æsthetic ' bric-à-brac group, the experimentalists, the realists and the decadents has never yet been fully acknowledged,

Meanwhile there will be the group of which I have just spoken as dealing in bric-à-brac, though each of its members had solider and more gravely wrought wares to offer. Dobson and Lang keep a tinge of Pre-Raphaelite colour; they go to France, not exactly in company with Swinburne, but on his hint; they follow up Swinburne's endeavour to use the fixed French forms; and they discreetly anticipate some later writers in their readiness to be occasional. With rarer gifts than are usually allowed them, both Dobson and Lang have a shrinking from the primary emotions, recoiling from the indelicacy of frank avowals, smiling away their emotions. Lang pays the full penalty of such timidity; his serious verse continually suffers from his refusal to recognize the real quality of his feeling. With Dobson the evasion results, at times, in a peculiar ironical pathos, strictly comparable with Watteau's, a pathos which is not in the words of Dobson's verse but without a perception of which he could not have written them. He goes to the eighteenth century to be, in his own shy way, very modern, and is well aware of the menace of a reality against the intrusion of which he erects such frail, gay defences.

The real decadence is delayed by this dexterous and innocent interlude, and by general realization that Tennyson, the alarms and excursions of the 'sixties and 'seventies being over, has reasserted his authority. But it is coming. The influences introduced by Swinburne, Baudelaire's, Gautier's influence, the suggestive criticism of Walter Pater, the pictures and paradoxes of Whistler, the attitudes of Oscar Wilde are having their effect. Henley, who is an art critic as well as a poet, both encourages and disguises the tendency. He is pathologically personal, in the sense of the phrase from Balzac which he prefixes to his hospital poems, and he is breaking up the larger poetic instruments in favour of an etcher's needle with which the strangest and most fugitive aspects of reality shall be noted. But he is also a bellowing, genial ruffian, easily taken for one of your hearty great fellows; and he will seem to go arm-in-arm with Mr Rudyard Kipling. They know better at the Café Royal, at the Rhymers' Club, in Vigo Street, and in the office of the enterprising and obscenity-loving Leonard Smithers. Oscar Wilde writes the best review of Henley's first volume of verse; Mr Arthur Symons writes the most discriminatingly enthusiastic estimate of Henley's verse as a whole, finding in it modernity becoming in a sense classical.

But it is an artist in line or paint that the period needs, its Rossetti: it finds two, Aubrey Beardsley, so eclectic that he seems to make himself equally out of Burne-Jones, Antonio Pollaiuolo, Japanese prints, Greek vase designs and contemporary French posters; and Charles Conder. And Victorian Romanticism ends in a distinguished perversity, in a kind of languid *fête galante*, as of that earlier Dobsonian entertainment grown complicated, ambiguous, here and there corrupt. It preserves some attitudes and costumes from the Rossetti period, it has some properties from Whistler, it has taken fans from Austin Dobson and masks from the earlier Verlaine and borrowed frippery in bulk from France, but its atmosphere, with that ' forgotten censer ' of Baudelaire perfuming it secretly, is its own. *Qualis artifex!* Victorian Romanticism is acutely aware that its end is at hand, and to be met in the spirit of the artist. *Fin de siècle* is murmured everywhere. All the books have been read, all the forbidden fruit eaten, and there is no need of Mallarmé to explain that the flesh is sad. But the final entertainment, religious in a way, has its carefully respected ritual. A great energy has been exhausted; there remain these rites, performed, for a change welcome to the weary epicures of sensation, *à rebours*. But the service of the Devil demands at least as much energy as the service of God, and only Beardsley seems to have known that truth.

The great outburst of Romanticism in France was followed by a reaction in which men attempted to reproduce the contemporary world, building, as the classic phrase has it, with bricks and mortar between the covers of a book, painting on no pretext from Byron or another poet, but with their eyes on the sobriety of nature and on the accidents of the human comedy. Nothing of the sort followed in England the suicide of Romanticism. How could it? Life had become, by then, too complicated, too full of things existing in satisfaction not of a universal and permanent demand, but of a transient requirement of a sophisticated society invaded by refined vulgarians. Realism, which even in France began to acknowledge its defeat when with Zola it took life in sections labelled ' Money,' ' Fertility,' or what not, instead of with the comprehensiveness of Balzac, was out of the question: contemporary life is too much for the writer who wishes neither to take it sectionally nor to hold a mirror to its general confusion. Realism is a phase, possible only for a period in which material things have begun to matter very greatly, but in which life is still co-ordinated and fairly simple. The future is with an expanded and courageous Romanticism, and in the inevitable revival the Victorian Romantics will once more have due

99

attention. Since they, with the exception of Morris, were specialists in imaginative experience, they may not mean as much to us as Blake and Coleridge and Shelley; but since they were more conscious of their ideals and more concentrated, they will have for us a peculiar value.

XXII

CONSIDER some of the ideas of Rossetti, whose every pronouncement has a peculiar note of authority. ' No imaginative artist,' he
tells us, ' can fully express his own tone of mind without sometimes
in his life working untrammelled by present reference to nature.'
But, he goes on, ' it is equally or still more imperative that immediate study of nature should pervade the whole completed work.'
And then, sharply dissociating himself from Holman Hunt's
practice and Ruskin's theory, by which, in its extremest and most
commonly quoted form,[1] painters are to go to nature and reproduce it, 'rejecting nothing, selecting nothing, and scorning nothing,'
he says finely:

Tenderness, the constant unison of wonder and familiarity so
mysteriously allied in nature, the sense of fullness and abundance
such as we feel in a field, not because we pry into it all, but because
it is all there: these are the inestimable prizes to be secured only
by such study (of nature) in the painter's every picture.

It is a very definite parting of company with Holman Hunt, who
would take an inventory of God's plenty where Rossetti bids us
refrain from prying into it all.

---

[1] It should always be remembered, however, as it scarcely ever is, that this is
Ruskin's caricature of his own teaching, excusable only because addressed to artists
in the making. His true position is indicated, in a passage already quoted in *The Stones
of Venice*. Ruskin's teaching ought, indeed, invariably to be studied with reference
to the occasion of its delivery, and with reference to all his other pronouncements on
the matter under discussion. But he has himself to blame if it is misunderstood.

What Rossetti thought of some contemporary painters and draughtsmen may be gathered from the passages he contributed to art criticisms by his brother; but it is more to our purpose to note his attitude towards two artists who in some ways link the work of Rossetti and his fellows to that of William Blake. Quite what he made of David Scott is not to be discovered. In the pages he wrote for Gilchrist's biography of Blake, Rossetti said that, despite claims rightly made for Etty and Maclise, ' David Scott will one day be acknowledged as the painter most nearly fulfilling the highest requirements for historic art, both as a thinker and a colourist,' since Hogarth. At times, however, Rossetti seems to have been perceptive enough of the defects and weaknesses of David Scott, and inclined to make jest of even those qualities by which he is in some sort of the tribe of Blake. About Samuel Palmer he had no doubt: ' Such a manifestation of spiritual force absolutely present—though not isolated as in Blake—has certainly never been united with native landscape-power in the same degree.'

But in regard to painting Rossetti very rarely reduced to precise statement the ideals he cherished; in regard to poetry he did so seldom, yet came much less short of covering the ground. His insistence on ' fundamental brainwork,' on ' mental cartooning,' his requirement that poetry should be as ' amusing ' as any other form of imaginative literature, that other requirement according to which ' poetry should seem to the hearer to have been always present to his thought, but never before heard ': these are utterances to be valued with Coleridge's, with those of Keats. I have already quoted that fundamental thing about poetry which he wrote to William Allingham. His criticism of poetry was entirely a poet's, which is why he estimated more highly than any but a poet will the poetry of Chatterton, of Wells, of Ebenezer Jones, of Hake, recognizing in immature or frustrate work an energy

The End of It.
(18th June. 1815.)

His brows met, and his teeth were set,
  And his mouth seemed in pain;
And madness closed and grappled with him
  As they turned his bridle-rein.
And albeit his eyes went everywhere,
  Yet they saw not anything:
And he drew the bit tightly, for he thought
  That his horse was stumbling.

There was a great shouting about him
  And the weight of a great din:
But what was the battle he had around
  To the battle he had within?
A pond in motion to the stress of the ocean
  A lamp to a furnace-eye,
Or the winds' wild weeping-fits
To the voice of Austerlitz
  When it shook upon the sky

Hark, hark, hark! through the spangled dark,
  To the left and to the right,
Hark, hark, hark! how the muskets bark
  Like ban-dogs heard at night:

While, the trumpet, all day shrill for blood
  Laughs with a cruel heave;
Ringing out fame and ringing in shame,—
  A peal for a New Year's Eve.

He ~~turned~~ stared right out, and he turned
        him about,
  And he knew that It must fall;
He knew the trodden ground for its bier
  And the cannon-smoke for its pall
Spurring, he gazed not back, but sped
  As speedeth the speedy wind
When, bound as far as St. Helena,
  It leaves Waterloo behind.

              =

              18th June. 1845.

which had need to produce more definite results for recognition by ordinary criticism. The pressing of the claims of exceptional art was congenial work for the whole group.

Rossetti, however pungent and stimulating his occasional remarks on painters and poets, did not anywhere bring to a head the dispute of his group with prevalent doctrine. That was done by Swinburne, who, with his personal message certainly, was in early years a voice for the group.

In 1858 Swinburne wrote a fragment of an essay on ' The Progress of Art in Modern Times,' which has not been published, and from the manuscript of which, in Mr Wise's collection, I quote some of the more significant sentences:

In most studies which have occupied men's attention there is a time of change, and a time of return to the elder models; men discover that those who were the first to introduce alteration were no nearer than their predecessors to judicial infallibility, and sometimes, in the reaction from one tone of thought or feeling, adopt too hastily the form which it originally superseded, or such a substitute as their own times may best be able to afford. In painting, as in other arts, this has been of late years the case, but among ourselves it has assumed a very different form from that which it had many years ago. . . . We do not, it is said, look upon art in the light in which its earliest apostles beheld it. Imitation, therefore, of the effects, when their causes are no more, can, if at all feasible, reproduce only a lifeless and servile copy, or a mannered caricature. To such men as Angelico, art and religion were indeed one; to call them indivisible was no mere form of words. Now this tone of mind we cannot re-attain; however desirable some may think it would be, we cannot transplant medieval feeling into the atmosphere of our daily life and work; we cannot reproduce it in painting or in writing, but only a dead unreal mockery of its outward tone.

This argument seems not very difficult to answer. Those who desire us to emulate the noblest models do not bid us sit down and copy them line by line. . . . Imitation, to be worth much, must begin from within and not from without. . . . The artist indeed must recur always to the same source of inspiration—not to any classical model ready made to order. It seems strange that a truism like this should at any time become a truth practically unrecognized; yet so it has been. Eyes long accustomed to consider the false and the factitious, real and faithful, looked upon genuine and beautiful truth, when it came before them, as unreal and absurd.

I interrupt quotation from Swinburne's boyish essay to recall that among such eyes were those not only of most of the accredited art critics of the period but of his adored Charles Dickens. If *The Times* described ' Christ in the House of His Parents ' as ' disgusting,' Dickens appreciated the early masterpiece of Millais in these terms:

In the foreground of the carpenter's shop is a hideous, wry-necked, blubbering, red-haired boy in a nightgown, who appears to have received a poke playing in an adjacent gutter, and to be holding it up for the contemplation of a kneeling woman, so horrible in her ugliness that (supposing it were possible for any human creature to exist for a moment with that dislocated throat) she would stand out from the rest of the company as a monster in the vilest cabaret in France or the lowest gin-shop in England.

But to resume quotation from Swinburne's essay:

Is not this indeed the heaviest misfortune which can happen to art, to be trammelled by factitious laws that no one understands or reasons out to their effect or traces to their natural source ? . . . But investigation does disprove the reasoning of such critics. In the sense in which they seem to use the word *imitation*—it is almost to say that Hunt or Millais imitates Perugino or Francia. It would be as absurd to deny the influence of those great painters who are usually classed together—somewhat vaguely—as Pre-Raphaelites.

All we can say is that, owing not a little to the influence of such studies, art among ourselves and elsewhere is growing ever into more of its pristine strength and purity; that the so-called *classical* style is waning, in art as in poetry; and that the great artists now living have taught us, and continue to teach us, that without truth no beauty can exist, and no good be gained by art or study.

So far, however, the quarrel is with the open enemy: presently it is with a supporter of the new group, with Ruskin, who has championed the Pre-Raphaelites, subsidized Rossetti and his wife, given private countenance to the audacity of the first ' Poems and Ballads ' of Swinburne himself.

As Carlyle had inculcated that the Fine Arts ' are sent here not to fib and dance, but to speak and work,' so Ruskin had tirelessly insisted on the morality of art: ' The duty of a painter is the same as that of a preacher'; ' it is the moral part of us to which Beauty addresses itself '; and so forth. To all of which Swinburne, with his own message and more of the moral rebel in him than his friends had, but still as their spokesman, retorted vigorously in the great book on William Blake:

Philistia had far better (always providing it be possible) crush art at once, hang it or burn it out of the way, than think of plucking out its eyes and setting it to grind moral corn in the Philistine mills.

With sharper vision in this matter naturally, but not without further sharpening of it by study of Gautier and Baudelaire and contact with Whistler, he had seen that the open enemies were less dangerous to art than the men who, ' unfit for service on either side,' halted for delivery of eloquent, conciliatory and confusing discourse between the camps in which art and morality are severally established. The Puritan, as he saw, is always in the right: right, and, for all his persecution of art, ultimately harmless. The really dangerous enemy is the middle-man ' with some admirable self-sufficient theory of reconciliation,' who clamours for art even more loudly than the artist, but will have it on conditions. The half-emancipated Puritan, afraid of his partial liberty, and justifying his fitful enjoyment of it by invocation of an authority which art cannot recognize: it is he who is the danger.

XXIII

ROSSETTI, in 1871, in reply to Buchanan, had his own pronouncement to make on morality and art, but there is little to our purpose
in *The Stealthy School of Criticism*. It is a defence, dignified and
persuasive, against libel by a man who had not thought out his
case against Rossetti or Rossetti's fellows; it is not a discussion of
fundamental problems. Two things in it, all the same, seem worth
quoting. The first is a comment on *Jenny*:

Neither some thirteen years ago, when I wrote this poem, nor
last year when I published it, did I fail to foresee impending charges
of recklessness and aggressiveness, or to perceive that even some
among those who could really *read* the poem, and acquit me on
these grounds, might still hold that the thought in it had better
have dispensed with the situation which serves it for framework.
Nor did I omit to consider how far a treatment from without might
here be possible. But the motive powers of art reverse the requirement of science, and demand first of all an *inner* standing-point.
The heart of such a mystery as this must be plucked from the very
world in which it beats or bleeds; and the beauty and pity, the self-
questionings and all-questionings which it brings with it, can come
with full force only from the mouth of one alive to its whole
appeal. . . .

As for the general accusation of fleshliness:

That I may, nevertheless, take a wider view than some poets or
critics, of how much, in the material conditions absolutely given
to man to deal with as distinct from his spiritual aspirations, is

admissible within the limits of Art—this, I say, is possible enough; nor do I wish to shrink from such responsibility. But to state that I do so to the ignoring or overshadowing of spiritual beauty is an absolute falsehood. . . .

It was, however, Swinburne in a like defence of earlier date, the ' Notes on Poems and Ballads,' who went to the root of the matter:

The question at issue is wider than any between a single writer and his critics, or it might well be allowed to drop. It is this : whether or not the first requisite of art is to give no offence; whether or not all that cannot be lisped in the nursery or fingered in the schoolroom is therefore to be cast out of the library; whether or not the domestic circle is to be for all men and writers the outer limit and extreme horizon of their world of work. . . . Who has not heard it asked, in a final and triumphant tone, whether this book or that can be read aloud by her mother to a young girl? Whether such and such a picture can properly be exposed to the eyes of young persons? If you reply that this is nothing to the point, you fall at once into the ranks of the immoral. Never till now, and nowhere but in England, could so monstrous an absurdity rear for one moment its deformed and eyeless head.

The morality of art, he says bluntly, is such that ' all things are good in its sight out of which good work may be produced.' The one fact for art which is worth taking account of is ' simply mere excellence of verse or colour, which involves all manner of truth and loyalty necessary to her well-being.' ' Her business is not,' he says in the *William Blake*, ' to do good on other grounds, but to be good on her own.' ' The contingent result ' of good art may be good living, ' but if the artist does his work with an eye to such results . . . he will too probably fail even of them.'

In all this there is something peculiar to Swinburne or derived by him from Gautier's preface to *Mademoiselle de Maupin* and

Baudelaire's criticism of Poe: the doctrine is too definite and too aggressive to be quite that of his friends. Yet in considering the work of the group, after Rossetti had separated himself from Holman Hunt and collected young disciples, we cannot but be aware of an unusual antinomianism, though it is only in part of Swinburne's own work and in some of Simeon Solomon's that we get to those 'subtle conspiracies of good with evil' which, under this aspect of the matter, are the characteristic of decadent art. One thing that must be noted is a peculiarity of Rossetti's. We know the manner of his life with Fanny Schott and the rest, and we know the language he and Swinburne and Howell habitually used, but whenever as an artist Rossetti has to touch on a certain evil he is like one who has heard no common or jesting term for it, seen none of its sorry comedy; he keeps that awed sense of it which awakes in a boy reading in the Bible simple and terrible words of the harlot.

XXIV

IN different ways and degrees Rossetti and William Morris and Swinburne are influenced by the old literatures to which they reach back, so that the doom upon their characters is Greek or Norse or Dantesque or out of Border ballads or out of Malory or out of the Bible itself, and not the contrived doom which the modern mind, fed on realistic fiction, expects. And if something of their attitude towards primary things must be referred back in this way, their styles must in great part be explained by reference to their translations and reproductions of old originals.

It has long seemed to me strange that so little importance has been attached by literary historians and critics to the models supplied by translations. All possible effects of the style of every great English writer in his original work on the styles of contemporaries and successors have been considered, to weariness, by genuine critics and by the writers of those intolerable academic theses which reach us daily from America. But that what an artist has done in translation may have had effects greater than any produced by his original work is not thought upon. Yet, as I have speculated elsewhere, the style of Dryden in his translations may have had much more than superficial effect on the style of FitzGerald in a paraphrase which owes little but substance and stanzaic form to Omar. In our own day we have seen, or might have seen if we had used our eyes, that the more elaborate manner of Mr Yeats in middle life is directly derived, not from the original lyrics of Mr Arthur Symons, but from that writer's translations of Mallarmé. And, to come to the point, it is plain that so far as Rossetti made

She came & looked against my bed & said:
Rise up & bind the shoes upon thy feet,
And thou shalt know of love, what thing is it,
And wherefore God made colours green & red.
So that I rose with feet uncovered
And gazed as one that hath a broken wit;
~~In the cool dark her face was vague & sweet~~
Who smells a rose & says it is not sweet
Because the ~~sake~~ this own sense feels disquieted.
Then I heard noises as of men at prayer,
And presently, ere one could breathe again,
She laid her hand across my face & prayed.
I saw behind the praying face of her
An angel standing ~~like a man~~ pale as one in pain
~~Whose lips seemed always with the words she~~ she said
~~And~~ But patient: so I knew that she was dead.

his style, it was in translating the early Italian poets, and that much in the early style of Swinburne was determined by Rossetti's translations.

Here is an unpublished early sonnet by Swinburne, written in 1858-9:

> The chosen angels and the happy dead
> That have in heaven their habitation sweet
> At the first passage of my Lady's feet
> In pity and wonder round her gatherèd.
> ' What light is this, what fair new thing? ' they said,
> ' For such fair presence and so full of grace
> Out of the wandering world to this high place
> Hath never all this age been carrièd.'
> To be in heaven is right great joy to her
> And stand among God's chosen holiest;
> Yet sometimes she turns back in very care
> To see me if I follow her to rest.
> Therefore my soul is always full of prayer
> Because I hear her pray me to make haste.

It is a translation from the Italian, and it is natural enough that Swinburne should have chosen to do it precisely in Rossetti's manner. But out of such things comes also the manner of nearly all the earlier of the *Poems and Ballads*, and a tinge of it clings to many even of the later poems of Swinburne.

Morris made his earlier style out of medieval models and out of the early work of Browning, so far as it was not wholly original, and then, rather late in life, was affected by his own Norse studies; but he too for a season, like everyone else who came in contact with Rossetti, was affected by that irresistible influence.

Common to the group are usages which have hardly yet been examined with enough intelligent care. The Pre-Raphaelites, always leaving the consummate Millais out of account, have been charged with faulty drawing; and it is plain enough that Rossetti in his impatience never learned to draw in the academic sense. But do not some of the peculiarities of the drawing in his work, in the early work of Burne-Jones, in that of most of the group, correspond significantly with certain peculiarities in the verse of such of them as were poets? Is it not suggestive that where Rossetti had complete mastery of the medium he yet took so many licences, especially in his weak rhymes? In him and in William Morris and in all the earlier, though not in the later, verse of Swinburne there is evidently a frequent deliberate use of weak rhyme or assonance or archaic and delaying constructions where these were easily enough to be avoided. The mimetic aim in a few of Rossetti's pieces and many of the earlier poems of William Morris and in the early deliberately Pre-Raphaelite poems of Swinburne and in his Border ballads explains a good deal, but not everything. Rhymes like that of ' love ' and ' thereof,' blank-verse endings like ' branches,' ' lute-player,' with many other obvious peculiarities of the group, combine to produce an effect closely comparable with that made by the tentative, mannered, slightly distorted drawing of the early work of some of these men and their friends.

Rossetti, approaching poetry as a painter, and until near the end of his life, when trouble with eye-sight forced him back on poetry, inclining to believe that the day of English poetry was nearly over whereas that of English painting was but dawning, naturally carries pencil and brush into his verse. William Morris, though not till his first and, as I think, strongest poetical inspiration was spent, habitually writes in the terms of the carver or weaver, so that his praise of a flower is in the epithet 'well-wrought.' Even Swinburne, in maturity the least pictorial of poets, has as critic a subtle appreciation of what in poetry may most nearly be the equivalent of graphic art, as may be seen on almost any page of his *William Blake*, and in the magnificent early eulogy of Baude-

laire, where he dwells on the excellence of that poet's ' drawing.'
But so far as there is ' drawing ' in the early poems of Swinburne
(there is none in work done after 1862), and whenever, which is
very often, there is ' drawing ' in Rossetti or in Morris, it is very
different from that which we find in Baudelaire. In the French
master, without becoming obtrusive, it is altogether helpful to
the poem as such; with those English poets, it is apt, whatever its
charm, to become a kind of illegitimate boon. Much of their work
is in one way or another overcharged: Rossetti's with design and
colour, Morris's with another kind of design, Swinburne's with
what it is convenient to call music, though, in fact, it is under
metrical rather than musical compulsion that he works. The poem,
strictly to be called such, comes to us not its bare self but as if
displayed in an illuminated manuscript, or on a tapestry, or,
in the case of Swinburne, with the throbbing of an appropriate
and marvellously sustained surplus of sound in that curious art of
over-tones.

XXV

THE forms most characteristic of this poetry while it was still Pre-Raphaelite or at least purely Romantic were fixed early, and by Christina Rossetti first of all. If in metrical science Swinburne surpassed all others in the group, as indeed all English poets, in instinctive metrical art Christina was his better. Look where you will in her verse, even at girlish work, and there is evidence of that freedom in service to the genius of the language which is the privilege of the perfect artist. In 'Goblin Market,' with its exquisite felicity of transition between the grotesque and the lovely, its queer enchantment of hopping, scrambling, faultless movements; in the song of songs in ' The Prince's Progress'; in ' Dreamland,' and ' Echo,' and ' Passing Away,' as in a host of minute poems made for mere child's play, there is a natural and infallible tightening and loosening of metre to which we shall find no parallel. But something in the early verse of Christina Rossetti is in some degree imitable, and there are the hints on which her brother made the cadences of some of his best lyrics and Swinburne fashioned certain of his stanzaic schemes. Moreover, though this is of slighter importance, Eleanor Siddal Rossetti, for all her absorption in Dante Gabriel, owes something to Christina. Take these verses by Mrs Rossetti, unpublished like all her work:

> I cannot give to thee the love
> I gave so long ago—
> The love that turned and struck me down
> Amid the blinding snow.

An Apple-gathering.

—

I plucked pink blossoms from mine apple tree
And wore them all that evening in my hair:
Then in due season when I went to see
    I found no apples there.

With dangling basket all along the grass
    As I had come I went the selfsame track:
My neighbours mocked me while they saw me pass
        me pass
    So empty-handed back.

Lilian and Lilias smiled in trudging by,
    Their filled basket teazed me like a jeer,
Sweet-voiced they sang beneath the sunset sky,
    Their mother's home was near.

Plump Gertrude passed me with her basket full,

34

A stronger hand than hers helped it along,
A voice talked with her thro' the shadows cool
  More sweet to me than song.

Ah Willie Willie, was my love less worth
 Than apples with their green leaves piled about?
I counted rosiest apples on the earth
  Of far less worth than love.

So once it was with me you stooped to talk
 Laughing and listening in this very lane
To think that by this way we used to walk
  We shall not walk again!' —

I let my neighbours pass me, ones and twos
 And groups; the latest said the night grew chill
And hastened: but I loitered, while the dews
  Fell fast I loitered still.
                      —— 23ʳᵈ November 1857.

I can but give a sinking heart
And weary eyes of pain,
A faded mouth that cannot smile
And may not laugh again.

Yet keep thine arms around me, love,
Until I drop to sleep:
Then leave me—saying no good-bye,
Lest I might fall and weep.

There is more of Mrs Rossetti's individuality in another piece,
'A Year and a Day,' which to me seems to announce a poet:

A silence falls upon my heart,
And hushes all its pain,
I stretch my hands in the long grass,
And fall to sleep again,
There to lie empty of all love,
Like beaten corn of grain.

If Dante Gabriel Rossetti was the master, it was William Morris
who in the early 'fifties gave the group the most readily imitable
models, affecting Swinburne a little later much more than
Rossetti did. For one thing, Morris was the discoverer of what
could be done with the stanza of three lines. There existed for
anyone hankering after such effects the familiarly known and
incomparable ' Dies Irae,' of which, it may be recalled, the youthful Swinburne made a version:

Day of wrath, the years are keeping,
When the world shall rise from sleeping,
With a clamour of great weeping!

And there were medieval English examples enough. But, as
regards such forms and the general obligation of the group to
medieval English poetry, it must be remembered that neither

Rossetti nor Swinburne was deeply read in the poetry which Wright and others had been editing during the 'thirties and 'forties, the astonishing scholarship of Swinburne in English poetry being that of a man but little interested in what was produced before, say, 1580. Archaism with Rossetti was either Italian or, if English, only incidental, a matter of a word or a refrain. The English archaic element in the work of the group was wholly Morris's. This is not very evident to those who think of Morris as the author of nothing earlier and cruder than the pieces in the great 'Defenceof Guenevere' volume, and of Swinburne as the author of nothing further from maturity than the few deliberately Pre-Raphaelite pieces in the first *Poems and Ballads;* but an examination of the earliest work of both, with due regard to the priority of Morris in date, leaves no room for doubt.

Morris, according to the legend, had the mastery of his instrument at first essay. There is the testimony of Richard Watson Dixon to the qualities of his very first composition, ' The Willow and the Red Cliff,' improvised in his twenty-second year, about two years before he met Swinburne: ' It was a thing entirely new, founded on nothing previous: perfectly original, whatever its value, and sounding truly striking and beautiful, extremely decisive and powerful in execution. . . . He reached his perfection at once.' And there is the poet's own remark, ' Well, if this is poetry, it is very easy to write.' Certainly, he has the mastery of his method in that other very early piece:

'Twas in Church on Palm Sunday,
Listening what the priest did say
Of the kiss that did betray,

That the thought did come to me,
How the olives used to be
Growing in Gethsemane.

That the thought upon me came
Of the lantern's steady flame,
Of the softly whispered name.

Of how kiss and word did sound
While the olives stood around,
While the robe lay on the ground.

Swinburne met Morris at Oxford at the beginning of November. He knew such things as Morris had published in the previous year in the *Oxford and Cambridge Magazine*, and now, having heard Morris recite certain other pieces, he at once began to write his own ' Queen Yseult ':

In the noble days were shown
Deeds of good knights many one,
Many worthy wars were done.

It was time of scath and scorn
When at breaking of the morn
Tristram the good knight was born.

Another very early piece by Morris, ' Blanche,' is duly echoed when Swinburne writes:

Then she prayed, if any heard,
And the air about her stirred
As the motions of a bird.

Morris, and the influence of Browning felt through Morris, and something of the mature Swinburne, are perceptible in a somewhat later Arthurian piece, also unpublished by him, which dates from 1859:

I love you now so well that verily
It were small pain if both of us were dead.

God leaves the latest rose some time to die;
Will He not leave us time to love and give
Sweet kisses—time to let my forehead lie
With your large hands to press the hair back? Live—
It seems so sad to live now; let us go
Into the church, and then may God forgive
If we lie down together and speak low,
The breath between your lips makes tremble mine—
And all these things will be forgotten so
And we shall die there, both of us—each line
Be straightened on that brow of yours, to leave
No wrinkle when the dumb white faces shine
Under the lighted altar. I believe
Christ would not let them hurt my Love being dead—
But you far up in Heaven would feel me grieve
And hear my heavy tears drop always, fed
With some new pain for ever, you would come
With a smooth aureole on your calm head,
Clothed round with solemn colours, and speak some
Strange word of comfort till I fell on sleep
With lips that trembled, passionate and dumb,
And woke to see—nay, sweet, you do not weep?

I dwell on such early work in *pastiche* because, more clearly than
the mature published work, it shows the interaction of these poets;
and I quote Swinburne because he was a greater master of *pastiche*
than either Rossetti or Morris. We shall see less of how Rossetti's
mind worked in his own early poems, before an exquisite art con-
cealed processes, than in such an imitation of him by Swinburne
as the piece entitled ' The Two Knights ':

The sea had wailed itself to sleep
Thro' clouds and blurrèd fire;
The sad moon seemed to shiver and weep
Like a thin face; but higher
Pure midnight made the stars seem deep
Fierce eyes of wild desire;

128

The Haystack in the Floods.

Had she come all the way for this,
To part at last without a kiss?
Yea had she borne the dirt and rain
That her own eyes might see him slain
Beside the haystack in the floods?

Along the dripping leafless woods,
The stirrup touching either shoe,
She rode astride as troopers do;
With kirtle kilted to her knee
To which the mud splashed wretchedly,
And the wet dripped from every tree
Upon her head and heavy hair,
And on her eyelids broad and fair
The tears and rain ran down her face.

By fits and starts they rode apace,
And very often was his place
Far off from her; he had to ride
Ahead, to see what might betide
When the roads crossed; and sometimes, when
There rose a murmuring from his men,
Had to turn back with promises;
Ah me! she had but little ease
And often for pure doubt and dread
She sobbed, made giddy in the head
By the swift riding, while for cold

K

or in:

> Six inches off the water-mark,
> The wet weed flaps in red,
> Fainter the sun's side, this way dark,
> As if some sea-beast bled
> Its heart out on those slabs of stone;
> The same sea-beast once whose spine
> Is now that rock's back, each bared bone
> A dry notch, bright with brine.

If we are looking, not to the value of the results, but to rigid fidelity to Pre-Raphaelite methods, it is the youngest and most mimetic of these poets that we must examine. But Swinburne hardly went too far when in later life he said that after 1860 he wrote nothing that could be called Pre-Raphaelite. Certainly by 1862 he had wholly abandoned imitation of Morris and Rossetti; and they themselves moved aside from the original course. A purely Pre-Raphaelite poetry, indeed, could have permanently contented no poet of the order to which they belonged. Its conventions would have constricted too severely any but a merely decorative poet, a lover of beautiful things rather than of beauty.

Each of them cared greatly for certain curiosities of beauty, but in their pronouncements on literature and art there are warnings enough against an exclusive passion for such things. Contemporaries might misunderstand some of their enthusiasm for the archaic, the exotic, but they were not what certain of their imitators became in the 'seventies and 'eighties.

XXVI

OF the effect which Rossetti and Swinburne had on critical opinion, in regard to particular men of genius, Villon, Blake, Fitz-Gerald, and others, there is little need to write. But they did more than establish such men in their due places; they altered the temper in which literature and painting were approached. A French writer produced a book on ' Ruskin and the Religion of Beauty,' and something must be allowed to Ruskin, in respect of the altered attitude towards painting at any rate. He was a great danger, with his confusions and prejudices, but he did beyond question create a public to which art, certain irrelevant requirements once satisfied, was a sacred thing. But these younger men, dismissing those moral or social sanctions—for the social argument with the William Morris of later days is not Ruskin's or conducive to any misjudgment of the intrinsic artistic worth of work—made art a thing sacred by its own virtue. In particular, the sensuous and technical elements of a work of art were now declared to be not matter for secondary appreciation, after its message had been taken to heart, but primary and on occasion all-sufficing. Here is the testimony of Rossetti:

Colour and metre, these are the true patents of nobility in painting and poetry, taking precedence of all intellectual claims.

Here is Swinburne's:

Art for Art's sake first of all, and afterwards we may suppose all the rest shall be added to her (or if not she need hardly be over-much concerned).

And with this new confidence in the absolute worth of art there

The Palace of Art

D. G. ROSSETTI

came in a new tone in writing of it. To read most of the criticism esteemed between the last writings of Lamb and the first writings of these men is to feel that works of art are being exposed to merely judicial or would-be judicial examination. There is a desolating lack of intimacy, of emotional response, there is not the least desire to do for books or pictures what Hazlitt did for certain poets when he reported his first experience of them. With Rossetti, in his few pages of critical prose, and still more with Swinburne, all that is changed. Their writing is not the vehicle of mere opinion: itself a work of art, the criticism presents to us a moving experience. With Swinburne especially criticism is a kind of passionate reminiscence, the eulogy inspired by a recent perusal of Hugo or Landor or an Elizabethan dramatist being coloured by memories of the shock of delight with which as a boy he encountered great work and first knew his kindred.

This, and the habit of estimating visible beauty which was naturally Rossetti's and which Swinburne acquired in the company of Rossetti and of Whistler and through his own prolonged study of Blake, affected the character of their prose. In another book I have shown that if there is any one passage in English prose whence Swinburne derived his, it is Charles Lamb's magnificent sentence in description of the 'Bacchus and Ariadne' of Titian; and earlier in the present book I have suggested that a certain sentence in Rossetti's 'Hand and Soul' was the model for many in Walter Pater. A comparison of passages in Rossetti's criticism of Blake, Swinburne's book on Blake and his essay on drawings by Old Masters at Florence, and the prose of Pater's *Renaissance*, will yield some curious results.

At the prose of Rossetti in 'Hand and Soul,' almost perfected in his first essay, a glance has already been taken. Here is a passage from his criticism of Blake which it would not greatly surprise one to find in Swinburne's study of the same master:

The tinting in the *Song of Los* is not, throughout, of one order of value; but no finer example of Blake's power in rendering poetic effects of landscape could be found than that almost miraculous expression of the glow and freedom of air in closing sunset, in a plate where a youth and maiden, lightly embraced, are racing along a saddened low-lit hill, against an open sky of blazing and changing wonder. But in the volume of collected designs I have specified, almost every plate . . . shows Blake's colour to advantage, and some in its very fullest force. See, for instance, in plate 8, the deep, unfathomable green sea churning a broken foam as white as milk against that sky which is all blue and gold and blood-veined heart of fire; while from sea to sky one locked and motionless face gazes, as it might seem, for ever. Or, in plate 9, the fair tongues and threads of liquid flame deepening to the redness of blood, lapping round the flesh-tints of a human figure which bathes and swims in the furnace. Or plate 12, which, like the other two, really embodies some of the wild ideas in *Urizen*, but might seem to be Aurora guiding the new-born day, as a child, through a soft-complexioned sky of fleeting rose and tingling grey, such as only dawn and dreams can show us.

The reader who fixes in his mind the facts that Rossetti's prose and Swinburne's are most nearly alike in their writings on Blake as a painter and designer, and that Pater, as Rossetti immediately pointed out in a letter to Swinburne, had a hint for the style of his essay on Leonardo from Swinburne's earlier published essay on drawing by Old Masters at Florence, and that Swinburne himself was so deeply affected as a writer of prose by Charles Lamb's eulogy of Titian, will have the solution of this problem. It is not that prose of this kind necessarily comes into existence with art criticism, which has as many instruments as criticism of literature, but that the attempt to expound painters of a peculiarly imaginative quality from within, to collaborate with them, to translate their work into words, produces with such writers, marked as are their differences, something that might be called a common language.

They are sufficiently unlike each other; but they are so much more unlike their predecessors and contemporaries, in this part of their work, that we are justified in emphasizing the points of their resemblance to each other. If there are at least two passages in Rossetti on Blake that would pass unquestioned by the average reader who should find them interpolated in Swinburne's study of that artist, there are at least three Swinburnian descriptions of drawings at Florence that might be taken for the work of Pater in some comparatively relaxed hour.

The critical influence of Rossetti, of Swinburne, of Pater, produced eventually a profound change in the way those choicer spirits of the age, the destined lovers of art, approached it. Under the Ruskinian dispensation, for all the genuine fervour and wonderful eloquence with which Ruskin pleaded for art, there were the confusions of an apologetic passion, justified by the moral worth of the beloved, cultivated, one might almost say, because the married are more useful members of society than the celibate, and finding excuse for its direction in all manner of irrelevant considerations. But here were men whose passion was for beauty simply as such, who most valued in art what was most strictly artistic, and who immortalized their experiences of beauty with as much ardour as ever went into the poetic memorial of a personal passion.

XXVII

HOLMAN HUNT'S attitude towards the English masters cannot be defined by any words but his own:

Those English artists who, since the commencement of their opportunities, have won honour for our nation, have firmly dared to break loose at some one point from the trammels of traditional authority. What gave the charm to Wilson's works was his departure from the examples of the classical painters whose general manner he affected. Wilkie, in his 'Blindman's Buff,' found no type of its sweet humour and grace in the Dutch masters; and Turner's excellence had no antecedent type of its enchantment in Claude or any other builder-up of pictorial scenery. Flaxman and Stothard are always most able in those works in which their own direct reading of Nature overpowers their obedience to previous example, and so it is with the best painters of our day. . . .

'We have, as an example of trammels, the law that all figures in a picture should have their places on a line describing a letter S— the authorities for convention finding the ground plan in Raphael's groups,' he writes, and we are reminded, not only of his own departures from that plan and from the pyramidical, but of the admirable daring of those early water-colours by Rossetti in which he worked on the diagonal, giving us in such a triumph as the 'Marriage of St. George' at once the 'dim golden dream' of Smetham's beautiful eulogy and firm geometrical design. Of the academic design against which Holman Hunt raged there is no better familiar example than Wilkie's 'Blind Fiddler,' since it both follows the S in the arrangement of figures and chief properties and the pyramid

and never stoop to pen
& ink — but I dare
say not a week goes
by without some such
letter.

And henceforth I'll try to
write in a more material
way.

Your affectionate
Ned

form in its grouping. But Wilkie had an observant and humorous eye as the typical Academician of his period had not, and the trouble was really not so much the **S** or the pyramid as the fear of all salient design, a fear which Rossetti did more to abolish than Holman Hunt. But all may share in the credit of having freely resorted to the forgotten colours purple and green and scorned the conventional gradation of colours. It is necessary, however, to be cautious in eulogy. With a fine sense of colours as they exist separately, Rossetti had not the least idea of what light does to them under certain conditions.

When Holman Hunt was instructing Rossetti and later, he was disconcerted by the younger man's ' independence of new life and joy in Nature,' and complained that ' Dantesque shapes of imagery' had become ' Rossetti's alphabet of art.' In 1851 it is Millais who says he wants to see in Rossetti's drawings ' a freshness, the sign of enjoyment of Nature direct, instead of quaintness derived from the works of past men.' Between Holman Hunt and Rossetti there long remained a personal bond. When Holman Hunt was leaving for the East, Rossetti gave him a daguerreotype of ' The Girlhood of the Virgin' with these lines from *Philip van Artevelde* written on it:

> There's that betwixt us been which men remember
> Till they forget themselves, till all's forgot,
> Till the deep sleep falls on them in that bed
> From which no morrow's mischief knocks them up.

But as artists they had drifted apart. As the result largely of Ruskin's misconception of the early history of the movement, Rossetti had been promoted not merely to a position of equality with Hunt and Millais in point of time but to leadership in genius. Actually, he had left Madox Brown without a notion of oil painting, and had needed seven months of assiduous tuition by Hunt to learn it, and had barely acquired it when he diverged in essentials from his colleagues of the P.R.B.; but in 1857 the *Athenæum* was found describing him as ' the original founder of the three-lettered race.' Generous minded as he was, Holman Hunt was not made happy by the exaltation, by friend and enemy alike, of a painter whom he had with only moderate success coerced and persuaded through the initial stages of oil-painting. Moreover, both Holman Hunt and Millais bore some excusable grudge against Rossetti for the zeal with which at the outset he had forced mediocre, *fainéant* or only half-converted members on the P.R.B., and Holman Hunt's feelings on this matter were probably strengthened when it was seen how well Rossetti had chosen when selecting such adherents for himself as William Morris, Burne-Jones and Swinburne. There was a display of jealousy by Rossetti at the Hogarth Club exhibition, whence he removed his own pictures as soon as Hunt managed to borrow for it his ' Two Gentlemen of Verona,' and there was continual irritation on the other side when ' Rossetti's undergraduate friends ' eulogized him without the least reference to the tardiness of his development. To Morris, Burne-Jones and Swinburne it naturally mattered not a jot that their regal friend had not so many years earlier been dependent on elementary instruction from Hunt, and that in precocity as a painter he had been immeasurably surpassed by the boyish Millais, but their praises wounded Rossetti's seniors. When it became known that Rossetti, bored by incessant chatter about the P.R.B., aware how far he had travelled on his own way since, and conscious of a portentousness which was quite absurd when the redeemers of Art were held to include the opportunist Millais, had dismissed the affair as little more than a youthful escapade, the breach was complete.

Long afterwards, in his candid, careful book, Holman Hunt argued out a case to which, in a sense, there was no answer. He overlooked the possibility that, if the movement was not that which

Rossetti represented, it might be so much the worse for the move-ment. The fine gifts and earnest intentions and courageous in-dustry of Holman Hunt, the swiftly attained technical mastery of Millais, cannot obscure the truth that there was in Rossetti a magnetic power which they did not possess. They attained, the one to be a kind of priest of art, the other to be the most popular of squires, getting an ample revenue out of pictures for huntin' and shootin', but Rossetti was the man born to be king. What Holman Hunt's argument implies is that 'Found' was Rossetti's first, and virtually his last, Pre-Raphaelite work. Well, 'Found' has among his graphic work the interest of 'Soothsay' among his poems. It proves, up to a point, that he was capable of working as a realist, and the poem proves that he could on occasion produce weighty gnomic verse. In each, Rossetti turns aside for a moment from his truest business. That in the picture he should have deviated from his natural course well after emergence from Holman Hunt's tutor-ship hardly helps Hunt's contention.

Of Ruskin's attitude towards Rossetti from about 1864, after a period of almost excessive admiration, it is difficult to write in measured terms. No man who ever lived has had the right to address to a man of genius, with whatever mitigating endearments, words of such insufferable patronage as we find in Ruskin's final letters. The assumption that it became him to decide the direction and limits of Rossetti's development and to lay down the con-ditions of a continuance of their friendship (' I will associate with no man who does not more or less accept my own estimate of my-self ') is ludicrous beyond laughter, and in the repeated assertion of his own superiority I find the very note of an irritated eunuch proclaiming his successes to Don Juan. Ruskin's financial generosity towards Rossetti and Mrs Rossetti had been extraordinary, but no services could excuse the peevish loftiness of that amazing series of epistles. Disconcerted and partly not comprehending, Holman

Hunt did willing justice to all in Rossetti's art that he could estimate and was silent or respectfully regretful about the rest. But Ruskin, without a fellow-artist's right of censure, offered Rossetti that worst of insults, of requiring him under threat to be other than his genius bade him be. Yet it was Ruskin who had striven, so wisely, to keep Rossetti to the early water-colours.

XXVIII

It may be doubted whether anyone in the circle or any outside sympathizer understood at the time how much was done by the illustrators to prepare a wider public for the painters. Those draughtsmen, of whom I have already taken critical notice, were associated, for the most part, not with a novel, difficult, æsthetically or morally questionable literature, but with accepted classics or with acceptable magazine fiction. No one, by laying particular stress on them, provoked attack on them. At first, some of them were not even allowed in the magazines to sign their names to their drawings. Unobtrusively, and often while dealing merely with contemporary life in its homely enough aspects, they pressed upon the public some of the characteristic merits of strictly Pre-Raphaelite or of Rossettian painting. Some opportunities were missed, and Moxon, the poets' publisher, missed two of the most important: he made too mixed a company of the illustrators of the Tennyson, and he lost his chance with Ford Madox Brown when the illustrations to the W. M. Rossetti edition of the English poets were under discussion. Here are some passages, showing a very just perception of the requirements of that enterprise, from a letter written by Brown:

It will be a repetition of the Illustrated Tennyson. Each artist thinking only of his own drawings, the whole will be, like that celebrated undertaking, wanting in that *ensemble* and uniformity so much required by the public in any work of the kind; and gradually the whole, growing beyond the publisher's first intention or powers of control, will either remain a continual hazardous worry on his hands, or have to stop short half-way of the goal. This, however, might be avoided by restricting the number of artists to a practicable limit; selecting them of a congenial turn of thought; and settling beforehand very strictly the size, nature, and style of the illustrations. I agree myself entirely with Payne's notion that wood-engraving publications have begun to pall upon the tastes of the more fastidious and intelligent of the public. The style of thing I would myself have proposed I intended should avoid the commonplace quality, by means of greater dignity and simplicity of style, and especially by a sustained uniformity of imaginative and intellectual faculty, versus the picturesque black-and-white dexterous unmeaningnesses that are now prevalent.

But it was little use preaching to publishers. The majority of those who issued the famous illustrated books and magazines of this period had no inkling of the greatness of the drawings that Millais, Sandys and their associates produced. Those drawings of the 'sixties have been increasingly honoured for the last thirty years, but one characteristic of them, their completeness, has often escaped attention. The most typical of them, and all of Rossetti's finished drawings, differ from the typical illustrations of the next generation and our own in being *pictures*, the surface filled as if it were canvas, the equivalent of colour contrasts and harmonies carefully supplied. It is not an art of making play with white spaces.

To return to my point, it was largely the work of the illustrators over that wonderful decade 1860-1870 which fitted the public as a whole to appreciate the painting of Holman Hunt, Millais, Rossetti and their friends and followers. With this must be taken into consideration the effect of the poetry of the Rossettis, Morris and Swinburne, of Swinburne's critical prose and of Walter Pater's, of the introduction of a small but influential body of readers to the sources whence Rossetti and his disciples, though not Hunt or Millais, drew much of their inspiration.

In rough suggestion of the position of the plain man before he was thus familiarized with the atmosphere, the properties and the methods of these artists, I will liken it, with due reserve, to that of a Frenchman witnessing the Romantic explosion without the least acquaintance, as regards art, with Constable, and, as regards literature, with Byron, Scott and the writers admired by Mme de Staël in her book on Germany. But the situation in France, in respect alike of art and literature, was much simpler. It would have been greatly simplified in England if the literary impact of the new Romanticism on the public could have preceded the excitement aroused by the painters. Again, it would have been simpler if Hunt, Millais and Rossetti had made a group more coherent and enduring. As it happened, of the seven original members four were virtually useless to the cause; and since Millais quickly cured himself of the imagination which was with him a contagious disease easily shaken off by so healthy a man, and Rossetti developed in his own direction, the battle had not long been joined when defection and confusion set in. The far more definable second or Rossettian phase yielded its own difficulties, but in it we do find cohesion; and the eventual complaints of Holman Hunt, natural as they were and free from pettiness of feeling, were not very reasonable. For it was inevitable that the more definite, the more sustained, movement should be recognized and the earlier, vaguer movement, in which only Hunt himself persisted, should be viewed, however erroneously, as no more than preparatory. 'The more sensuous phase of taste developed in Rossetti's later period was of hothouse fancifulness, and breathed disdain for the robust, out-of-door growth of native Pre-Raphaelitism.' No doubt; but if the mature Rossetti could not be the leader of the Pre-Raphaelites because he was no longer really of them, he was a leader nevertheless, and of a movement more profoundly affecting those whom it touched at all than Pre-Raphaelitism.

The true line of attack is not that Rossetti, in part falling short of the Pre-Raphaelite ideal, presently diverged to serve another, but that he and his disciples were never in the fullest sense painters. In his rejection of so much of the material of the greatest painters, in his discontent with the utmost significance that most of it, however imaginatively seen, can properly have and his resolve to charge the picture with all that his most packed sonnet might hold, even more than in his technical limitations, Rossetti was not of the race of the greatest painters. It is not merely that he was the painter, as he was the poet, of mystery. The mystery of the flesh exists for every great artist, but with the supreme masters of painting it is educed from a frank record, and with Rossetti it is not. He paints the woman, in his sister's words, ' not as she is but as she fills his dream.' ' And what, Mr Rossetti,' asks Jowett in Max's cartoon, ' would they have done with the Holy Grail when they had found it ? ' But Rossetti might be asked questions less impertinent.

XXIX

THE history of the reputation of the Rossetti circle cannot leave any student of it with the happy feeling of one who observes a natural, timely, steady growth to due height.

I have earlier suggested that the poets of his group might have come before the general public with a substantial body of work acceptable by all intelligent readers some years earlier than in fact they did. I propose now to examine the stages of their unlucky emergence.

The periodical of broad appeal, taking the verse of a new poet into quarters where neither his nor any new verse would ordinarily enter, is obviously the best instrument of introduction. Well, we find no major member of the group contributing to any but a short-lived coterie periodical till, in 1862, Swinburne writes for the *Spectator*. Swinburne is then twenty-five, Rossetti thirty-four; the one not too young to have issued some slim volume of lyrical verse, the other old enough to have achieved high poetic fame. Actually, they have given even the restricted public by the end of 1862 no more than what is contained in this brief list:

Dante Gabriel Rossetti
  I. ' Sir Hugh the Heron.' Privately printed. 1843.
  II. Sonnet, ' This is that blessed Mary, pre-elect.' Catalogue of the Free Exhibition of Modern Art. 1849.
 III. Contributions to the *Germ*, already noted.
 IV. Contributions to the *Oxford and Cambridge* magazine, already noted.
  V. *The Early Italian Poets*. 1861.

Algernon Charles Swinburne

  I. 'Congreve.' *Imperial Dictionary of Universal Biography*. 1857.
  II. Contributions to *Undergraduate Papers*, already noted.
  III. *The Queen Mother Rosamond*. 1860.
  IV. 'The Fratricide.' (Reprinted as 'The Bloody Son,' when Swinburne unfortunately changed 'I hae but anither' into 'I hae not anither,' though the mother cannot know till the climax that she has now no other son.) *Once a Week*. 1862.
  V. The following contributions to the *Spectator*: (1) 'Victor Hugo's New Novel'; (2) 'A Song in Time of Order'; 'Before Parting'; (3) 'After Death'; (4) 'Faustine'; (5) 'Mr George Meredith's " Modern Love "'; (6) 'Les Misérables'; (7) 'A Song in Time of Revolution'; (8) 'The Sundew'; (9) 'August'; (10) 'Charles Baudelaire: " Les Fleurs du Mal "'; (11) 'Victor Hugo's Philosophy.'

William Morris, in a sense, does not come into the argument. The *Defence of Guenevere* volume contained, as I have said earlier, some of the greatest, certainly the most intense, poetry he ever produced. But it was too sudden an attack on the public. Heeded by few, it disconcerted most of those few. And Christina Rossetti made her way to fame with work which, often closely akin to her brother's, yet seemed to recommend itself by qualities not perceptibly present in his poetry or in that of Morris or in that of the youthful Swinburne. The last-named, by choosing to appear before the wider public with two plays on models little known to it, instead of with lyrics, had done nothing in 1860 to advance himself or his friends. *Atalanta* was a success remote from the common course, wholly misleading to readers who looked to subject and

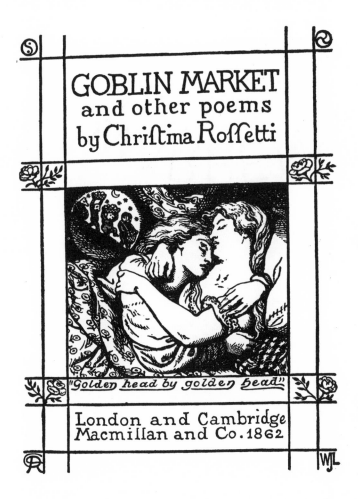

GOBLIN MARKET
and other poems
by Christina Roſſetti

"Golden head by golden head"

London and Cambridge
Macmillan and Co. 1862

machinery rather than to the inner spirit. And then came the distracting sensation of the first *Poems and Ballads,* with scandal and irrelevance. Rossetti's original volume was some years too late to be received in the right temper, to be regarded as other than a precious curiosity of beauty or a further manifestation of artistic carnality. And with the æstheticism promoted by Oscar Wilde there was yet more confusion of issues.

In time all this will cease to matter; but it matters still. Misunderstanding, scandal, cult, craze, but hardly anywhere, for perhaps thirty years, an honest and sensitive submission to artistic experience: could anything be more harmful to the fame of a group of poets? And since the painters could best be appreciated if men came to them through the poetry of the group, could there be much worse luck for a group of painters?

Perhaps, yes; and the curse of that possibly greater evil was on them. Fortunate is the artist in any kind who, like Wordsworth, has to be loved before he seems worthy to be loved; thrice fortunate the artist, like Walter Savage Landor, who is independent of the love of all not born to love him, who raises no heat of admiration on casual encounter and lives on unscanned save by eyes that revere him permanently. These others, in their eventual success, took captive many soon to be ransomed or to escape.

They were not spared the embarrassment of disciples. Now, it is commonly said that no great man is to be blamed for his followers, but is that strictly true? Is there not something the matter with work which stimulates a cult as Rossetti's did? I do not suggest that the Gongorism or Marinism of certain writers in the late 'seventies or in the 'eighties can be matched in the verse of Rossetti at his worst, or that the attitudes and decorative schemes of the ' æsthetic ' period can be justified out of the work of Rossetti as a painter and Morris as a designer. But the group did leave itself open to misunderstanding and afford pretexts for preciosity.

' Æstheticism ' and its products have long been discredited, but the work of the masters has not been wholly freed from somewhat sickly associations. It is not yet a safe assumption that a man who names Rossetti with reverence has in mind the concentrated power of his imagination; there is still the possibility that he may be seeing in Rossetti only what Wilde saw in him. He who salutes Swinburne to-day may be doing so only out of a memory of the fever Swinburne's most boyish verse put into his blood as a boy. There still hangs over the whole situation the suspicion that admiration of the group may be an admiration of beautiful things rather than of beauty.

Of all the arts, it is literature that lies in greatest peril of a misunderstanding by which the means may be admired without perception of the end, and the words which are really no more to the writer than colours to the painter or the separate notes to the musician be promoted to an undue importance. But painting, in the degree to which it becomes literary, becomes liable to the same danger. Here are certain artists in poetry and painting intensely concerned that the means, the accessories, should be beautiful in themselves, not only as instruments of a beautiful purpose; and who shall blame them? There are other ways of working, to not less beautiful and perhaps broader purposes; but this method is lawful and delightful. It happens, however, that they tend to choose the archaic, the exotic, the means and accessories that are curious as well as beautiful. One seems almost wholly medieval, another decadent; all speak a language in part foreign or antique, to tell us, as it seems, only of what is remote from common experience. What more natural than that stress should be laid enthusiastically on all this for a while, and that later on, in revulsion from a cult little recommended by its promoters, these artists should be dismissed to comparative neglect?

But the genuine critic, however closely he may study the ways by which an artist approaches beauty, is ultimately concerned only with results. Archaic or contemporary, what matter the language so that the thing to be expressed is finely expressed? Morality or antinomianism, what matter so that the end be attained? As between age and age, and as between individuals in each age, there will be preferences, of no profound æsthetic importance, for accessories of one sort over accessories of another, but they are only accessories, and the wisdom of the artist is wholly in choosing those which enable him, with his proper powers and limitations, to render his peculiar experience of beauty.

So it is that much subsequent disparagement of the work of Rossetti and his fellows is but the error of the ' æsthetes ' inverted. And if there was spiritual snobbery in those who got a compendiously condensed ' culture ' out of the Pre-Raphaelites, valuing them chiefly for that reason, there is no less in the endeavour to acquire merit by rejecting the Pre-Raphaelites.

In the popular and in the self-consciously ' intellectual ' view of these matters, it is assumed that there is some method of getting past an artist to his sources, of tapping directly for ourselves or indirectly through other artists, more congenial to us at this hour, the reality on which the demoded artist drew. But nothing of the sort is possible. There is no way of direct access, and there is no substitute means of enjoying experience of a reality existing apprehensibly only in the particular forms in which Rossetti and his associates offer it to us. It is not merely that in their originally almost complete and even to the end considerable ignorance of early painting Rossetti and his friends had an unhistorical idea of painting before Raphael. That was only an accident. It is that Rossetti's thoroughly studied early Italian poets became in his renderings of them Rossetti's, that the medieval world of William Morris was Morris's, that the Greece and France and Elizabethan England of Swinburne were Swinburne's, and that the only method of getting to the reality of each is to study Rossetti, Morris, Swinburne. And so with the vision each had of the contemporary world, and of what is permanent in life: it reveals realities apprehensible only in the colours or words with which these artists made their patterns. To turn away from them is to turn away from our only opportunity of seizing what doubtless has been and ever will be part of life but is seizable only in their embodiments of it.

It is by this activity of grasping things isolated from the chaotic flux and made significant that we live, with art as the prime necessity even for those who are unaware of it. And though we may reasonably argue the superiority, or at least the wider utility, of such art as presents to us, amply and soberly, the most readily recognizable realities, we must also pause to reflect that the art which seems most nearly the experience common to us all might better, for that very reason, suffer the loss of a few individual practitioners of it than an art presenting us with remoter, subtler realities. Not that we can really spare the least work of art in any kind! But suppose Poe, Baudelaire, FitzGerald (as Omar) dropped out of knowledge, and the literature of the nineteenth century is disproportionately impoverished. Watts, who tried, too often with success, to speak a language that would have been equally comprehensible in the studios of all the great ages and centres of painting, might be better spared than Whistler, in many ways the smaller artist, and it does seem to me many groups of highly gifted painters, with more of the specific quality of painters, might leave us less poor in their disappearance than the Pre-Raphaelites in their expulsion.

But in all such matters one can do little more than judge personally. The catholicity which his clients expect of the auctioneer is not desired in anyone else. One makes one's self, unconsciously, out of experiences of beauty, all valuable, all arousing gratitude, but some more to one's private purpose, when that manifests itself, than others, and there results a certain bias. Yet, whatever value may be set on what the Pre-Raphaelites give us, it will not be disputed that they have their specific qualities not as mere adjuncts but in the law of their being.

THE END

INDEX

INDEX